OBSESSIVE COMPULSIVE ANONYMOUS

Recovering From Obsessive Compulsive Disorder

Obsessive Compulsive Anonymous, Inc.
New Hyde Park, New York

ISBN: 0-9628066-0-9
Library of Congress Catalog Card No.: 90-92108

First Printing 1990
Second Printing 1992

DESIGNED AND PRINTED BY
ALDEN GRAPHICS LTD.
BOX 307
WILLISTON PARK, NEW YORK 11596

Table of Contents

Acknowledgment

We would like to thank Alcoholics Anonymous (A.A.) for allowing us to adapt their Twelve Steps and Twelve Traditions for Obsessive Compulsive Disorders. Their help and cooperation from the start has made our road smoother.

This time-tested program, detailed in *"Alcoholics Anonymous"*[1] and *"Twelve Steps and Twelve Traditions"*[2] has brought recovery for thousands of alcoholics. Patterning Obsessive Compulsive Anonymous after A.A. has also brought recovery among us. What follows is Obsessive Compulsive Anonymous' experiences with the Twelve Step program and not those of A.A.

Our personal stories are included in the hope that those reading them might benefit as much as we who have written them.

[1] *Alcoholics Anonymous* (New York: A.A. World Services Inc., 1976).
[2] *Twelve Steps and Twelve Traditions* (New York: A.A. World Services Inc., 1981).

Foreword

Obsessive Compulsive Anonymous (OCA) is a fellowship of people who share their experience, strength and hope with each other that they may solve their common problem and help others to recover from Obsessive Compulsive Disorder (OCD). The only requirement for membership is a desire to recover from OCD. There are no dues or fees; we are self-supporting through our own contributions. OCA is not allied with any sect, denomination, politics, organization or institution; does not wish to engage in any controversy, neither endorses nor opposes any causes. Our primary purpose is to recover from OCD and to help others.*

We choose to remain anonymous at the public level for several good reasons. Anonymity allows us to share our personal stories, knowing that they will remain in the confidence of those who attend our meetings. Anonymity also reinforces that it is the program, not the individual, that is responsible for the recovery.

We hope that by publishing a book of this kind others with OCD will read it and conclude that OCA can also work for them. The recovery program, clearly explained in the following pages, when incorporated into our lives, produces the desired changes which substantially relieves our obsessive-compulsiveness.

If you are alone you may feel afraid that you really can't do this — that it is too much to ask. Remember that it takes only this book and two people with OCD to have a meeting. We have found each other through many avenues and in time you will find others who want this program. We are no longer alone.

* The Preamble adapted with permission of the A.A. Grapevine Inc.

What is Obsessive Compulsive Disorder?

Here we provide the current Diagnostic and Statistical Manual of Mental Disorders, Third Edition, Revised, definition of OCD. We hope the reader will get a general idea of what our symptoms appear to be. If the following description does not seem to fit you - don't be concerned. Perhaps the remainder of the text will strike some familiar chords. All are welcome at our meetings if they think they may belong.

*Obsessive Compulsive Disorder (or Obsessive Compulsive Neurosis). The essential feature of this disorder is recurrent obsessions or compulsions sufficiently severe to cause marked distress, be time-consuming, or significantly interfere with the person's normal routine, occupational functioning, or usual social activities or relationships with others.

Obsessions are persistent ideas, thoughts, impulses, or images that are experienced, at least initially, as intrusive and senseless - for example, a parent having repeated impulses to kill a loved child, or a religious person having recurrent blasphemous thoughts. The person attempts to ignore or suppress such thoughts or impulses or to neutralize them with some other thought or action. The person recognizes that the obsessions are the product of his or her own mind, and are not imposed from without (as in the delusion of thought insertion).

*Reprinted with permission from the *Diagnostic and Statistical Manual of Mental Disorders, Third Edition, Revised.* Copyright 1987 American Psychiatric Association.

The most common obsessions are repetitive thoughts of violence (e.g., killing one's child), contamination (e.g., becoming infected by shaking hands), and doubt (e.g., repeatedly wondering whether one has performed some act, such as having hurt someone in a traffic accident). *Compulsions* are repetitive, purposeful, and intentional behaviors that are performed in response to an obsession, according to certain rules, or in a stereotyped fashion. The behavior is designed to neutralize or to prevent discomfort or some dreaded event or situation. However, either the activity is not connected in a realistic way with what it is designed to neutralize or prevent, or it is clearly excessive. The act is performed with a sense of subjective compulsion that is coupled with a desire to resist the compulsion (at least initially). The person recognizes that his or her behavior is excessive or unreasonable (this may not be true for young children and may no longer be true for people whose obsessions have evolved into overvalued ideas) and does not derive pleasure from carrying out the activity, although it provides a release of tension. The most common compulsions involve hand-washing, counting, checking, and touching.

When the person attempts to resist a compulsion, there is a sense of mounting tension that can be immediately relieved by yielding to the compulsion. In the course of the illness, after repeated failure at resisting the compulsions, the person may give in to them and no longer experience a desire to resist them.

Associated features. Depression and anxiety are common. Frequently there is phobic avoidance of situations that involve the content of the obsessions, such as dirt or contamination. For example, a person with obsessions about dirt may avoid public restrooms; a person with obsessions about contamination may avoid shaking hands with strangers.

Age at onset. Although the disorder usually begins in adolescence or early adulthood, it may begin in childhood.

Course. The course is usually chronic, with waxing and waning of symptoms.

Impairment. Impairment is often moderate or severe. In some cases acting according to the compulsions may become the major life activity.

Complications. Complications include Major Depression and the abuse of alcohol and anxiolytics.

Predisposing factors. No information.

Prevalence. Although the disorder was previously thought to be relatively rare in the general population, recent community studies indicate that mild forms of the disorder may be relatively common.

Sex ratio. This disorder is equally common in males and in females.

To Those of Us Who Are "New" to Obsessive Compulsive Disorder

It seems that OCD has received much attention of late. Almost everywhere we turn there is some news program or magazine article about our problem. For some of us, finally accepting that *this* was our problem was a source of comfort after years of confusion.

Unfortunately, many of us were led to believe that we were somehow responsible for getting OCD or that if we weren't so "weak" we would be better already. At OCA we were then told that we were not responsible for getting OCD but that we *were responsible* for working toward our recovery.

At this writing, the medical and psychological communities appear to have effective treatments for OCD. OCA does not endorse any specific treatments for OCD but *we do recommend our members see a doctor skilled in the diagnosis and treatment of OCD*. Resources* can be contacted for referrals to a professional in your area. OCA is *not* a referral center or a psychological counseling service.

OCA *is* a fellowship of people who are using the 12-Step program to obtain relief from our obsessions and compulsions. We have found that by incorporating the suggestions in this book into our lives we are granted significant relief from our OCD. Those of us at OCA who are receiving professional help for OCD have found this program a welcome addition.

---

*A full list of resources can be found on the last page of this book.

What follows are endorsements from professionals who feel that what OCA has to offer can prove beneficial for the OCD sufferer.

Twelve Step Programs and Obsessive Compulsive Disorder: A Note to Mental Health Professionals

Watching a person struggling with Obsessive Compulsive Disorder (OCD) is something like watching an alcoholic trying to fight his disease. In each case, the person may go through alternating phases of the struggle — sometimes trying to fight, control or defeat the compulsion through will power, and at other times denying to himself that any problem exists, even though he might be suffering from serious problems in regard to self-esteem, guilt, interpersonal relationships, and job functioning caused by the disorder. Another similarity between the two disorders is that both are very difficult to treat and some people with these problems have tried many different treatments with little improvement.

The twelve-step program of Alcoholics Anonymous has helped many alcoholics to recover from their disease and to achieve sobriety. The twelve steps have also been used by other self-help groups for various compulsive and addictive problems, including compulsive eating and compulsive gambling. Recently, a new self-help group, Obsessive Compulsive Anonymous (OCA), has started using the twelve steps to help people with OCD. Although it is too early to evaluate the effectiveness of this program, as of this writing (January, 1989), several people in my area have already been helped to greatly reduce their symptoms.

I do not see OCA as a competitor of psychotherapy, behavior therapy, or medication. Rather, I believe that an eclectic, pragmatic, empirical approach to the treatment of OCD can include each of these treatments. One combination of techniques may work better with one individual, while another combination may work more effectively with a different person. For some people, a self-help group such as OCA may be very useful either by itself or in conjunction with psychotherapy, behavior therapy, and/or medication. Research and additional clinical experience will be needed to specify more clearly which approaches work best for which individuals.

For mental health professionals who are unclear as to how or why the twelve-step groups help people, Gregory Bateson (1972)[3] and Robert Arnold (1977)[4] have written articles that analyze the psychological mechanisms through which these programs work. These mechanisms include group support, empathy and concern, specific cognitive techniques to reduce anger and anxiety, identification with people who are successfully recovering from the problem, a spiritual awakening or rebirth, acceptance of the reality of the problem and acceptance of other aspects of reality that were previously denied, restructuring of the individual's personality and character defenses, development of ego strength, an improvement in self-image, improvement in interpersonal relationships, gaining the ability to trust other people, giving up the need to control and manipulate other people, accepting responsibility for one's own life, and overcoming feelings of shame and worthlessness.

[3] Bateson, G. (1972). *Steps to an Ecology of the Mind*. New York: Ballantine.
[4] Arnold, R.J. (1977). A.A.'s 12 steps as a guide to "ego integrity." *Journal of Contemporary Psychotherapy, 9*. 62-77.

While mental health professionals working with OCD patients may not accept every aspect of the twelve-step programs, there is no inherent incompatibility between a self-help program based on the steps and most psychotherapeutic approaches. At this point in time, I would suggest an objective attitude on the part of professionals toward OCA and the twelve steps, as clinical experience begins to accumulate.

By Douglas R. Hogan, Ph.D.
Clinical Psychologist
Garden City, New York

A Place For Us

"Where Healing Begins With Love"

P.O. Box 720895
Orlando, Florida 32872-0895
(800) 543-3662

Diseases and symptoms aren't really the problem. They're actually the body-mind's attempt to solve a problem — a message from the subconscious to the conscious.

Many traditional medical practitioners are concerned with chipping away at surface needs, merely treating and eliminating the evidence of disease. And, while this is important, it's not enough! The real source for disease lies buried deep beneath the surface.

Real, permanent recovery takes place in the program Obsessive Compulsive Anonymous. OCA encompasses a process of awareness, education and growth, utilizing the twelve step model of Alcoholics Anonymous. It works!

Recovery is never a static state. There are many degrees to the process of recovery, just as there are degrees of illness. Recovery is more than the mere absence of symptoms.

Obsessive Compulsive Anonymous offers hope to the suffering, giving a sense of identification and a knowledge that you aren't alone anymore! Members share their experience, strength and hope through living testimonials. The sense of belonging plus acceptance that members experience becomes the first step *out* of their disease.

Obsessive-compulsives attempt to control their lives by setting excessive routines and rituals that lead to predictable experiences. It's like the unhappy marriage that I describe as "comfortable misery" — so predictable and less threatening.

Many obsessive-compulsives were raised in unpredictable home environments or are currently involved in relationships full of unpredictability. They are able to plan, follow through, and predict how they'll feel after each ritualistic episode.

It's the routineness and reliability of the ritual that is important. But the avoidance of spontaneous feelings impedes the development of intimate relationships and it becomes a disease of *isolation* similar to other addictions.

OCA becomes the process of recovery. It enables members to handle the stress and emotions of everyday life. Healing takes place through a physical, emotional, and spiritual solution which empowers its members with a personal strength beyond explanation.

The twelve steps of recovery, within a non-judgmental fellowship, enable OCA members to live in the "now," one day at a time, knowing they don't have to be perfect. Members feel a definite lessening of restrictions and rules, and learn to trust themselves and others.

That chain of one obsessive-compulsive helping another is spiritual in itself and, in my opinion, provides the essential component for this aspiring fellowship. To quote a phrase of AA, "It's the love of the fellowship that gets you sober; and it's the 12 steps that keeps you sober."

Obsessive Compulsive Anonymous creates the pathway to serenity. Self-responsibility and love are the foundations in the pursuit of balance and integrity.

WILMER C. BETTS, M. D.

GENERAL PSYCHIATRY
ADDICTIONOLOGY

920-A PAVERSTONE DR.
RALEIGH, N. C. 27615

March 12, 1990

Obsessive Compulsive Anonymous
P.O. Box 215
New Hyde Park, NY 11040

Dear Fellowship of OCA:

I want to thank you for your kindness in sending me the draft of the Obsessive Compulsive Anonymous organization manual.

I read it with considerable interest and want to congratulate you and your colleagues for the creation of the very excellent publication. I have been referring my patients with OCD to a 12 Step Recovery Program for some 6 years. I feel that a spiritual program structured by the 12 Steps is a realistic adaptation to any chronic illness. I send my best wishes for every success in achieving publication of your "Big Book."

With kindest regards, I remain

Sincerely yours,

Wilmer C. Betts, M.D.

WCB/gfb

Thomas E. Lauer, M.D.
Diplomate in Psychiatry

High Point Medical Center
624 Quaker Lane, Suite A-111
High Point, North Carolina 27262

February 19, 1990

Obsessive Compulsive Anonymous
Post Office Box 215
New Hyde Park, New York 11040

Dear Fellowship of OCA:

It has been my experience in working with individuals who are in recovery from chemical dependency to recognize that the addiction model shares much with obsessive compulsive disorder. Specifically, we see in alcoholics the mental obsession to drink, followed by the first drink, and the subsequent onset of compulsive drinking. This tends to be even more significantly seen in the use of other potent mood altering chemicals such as Heroin and Cocaine. Indeed we even recognize that in certain affective disorders, e.g., manic depressive illness, that the onset of a manic episode produces a pleasurable stimulus for the individual, a resulting desire to continue with that pleasurable stimulus, and indeed an escalation into full blown mania, this being quite out of control.

It is also true from my experience, that the individual with obsessive compulsive disorder becomes involved in certain obsessions, finding their ultimate relief only in carrying out their ritualistic compulsive behaviors.

For those of us familiar with the spiritual aspects of mental health it is quite clear that many individuals will respond very positively to a 12 step recovery program. This is particularly true if a person can become honest, open minded, and willing to change. The ultimate surrender of the individual with obsessive compulsive disorder, and the involvement in a spiritual program of recovery will be successful in virtually every case for those who persevere.

I strongly endorse the program of Obsessive Compulsive Anonymous for anyone who is seeking recovery from their obsessive compulsive disorder.

Yours sincerely,

Thomas E. Lauer, M.D.
TEL/bh

Spirituality for a Twelve Step Program for Compulsive and Obsessive Behavior

by Father Leo Booth

It is often said, and said with enthusiasm, that the key to recovery from addiction, compulsive and obsessive behavior, is spirituality. Most treatment centers and therapy agencies are concerned to stress spirituality as an important aspect of recovery. All Twelve Step programs are spiritual, basing themselves on the "spiritual awakening" that enables continual recovery as a daily basis.

But what is spirituality? For many people (although not everyone) it is easier to spell than explain. Indeed spirituality is often a cause of anger and debate, often confused with religion. Obsessive-compulsives are sometimes reluctant to embrace a program that might be considered suspiciously religious in nature — especially if they or their parents have suffered ridicule, condemnation and ostracization at the hands of ministers, priests or rabbis. I would like to suggest that this "key to recovery," this important aspect of wellness is often the source of confusion, not least amongst professionals: perhaps for this reason spirituality is mentioned and emphasized rather than explained!

In this article I shall seek to explain spirituality and apply it to the treatment and on-going recovery programs for compulsive and obsessive people. In my book "Spirituality and Recovery: A Guide to Positive Living," I defined spirituality as being that God-given ingredient (given to *all* human beings, regardless of color, culture or creed) that enables the development of a positive and creative lifestyle. Spirituality is the activated outcome of being made in the image of God. Spirituality reminds us that we were created to create. Therein lies our responsibility. My understanding of spirituality is not simply seen in placing our future dependency upon a Higher Power, but rather stresses an understanding of spirituality more as a precious gift from God that requires nurturing and nourishment. We are responsible for the development of spirituality in our lives.

Spirituality is also not just concerned with prayer and meditation, although I understand that we can give a broad definition of both these topics. Spirituality is concerned with the WHOLE human being; that involves the body, mind and emotions. If it really is true that God does not make junk then this comprehensive approach to spirituality makes incredible sense. It also absorbs all the various aspects of the treatment modality and recovery agencies into its catchment: doctors, clergy, nurses, therapists, nutritionists, physiotherapists, counselors, sponsors and fellow members of a Twelve Step group. In other words all those who are involved in developing a positive and creative life-style are involved in this dynamic concept of spirituality.

How does this definition help those suffering from a dysfunctional, obsessive and compulsive behavior pattern? Well it clearly reminds the sufferers that they need to be involved in their healing, their recovery. To believe in a miracle is to understand that you *are* that miracle. Spirituality involves developing and maintaining a change in attitude and behavior. Perhaps when Adam and Eve sought an answer to their human problems in the forbidden fruit from the tree (so they could be "as God") obsessive and compulsive behavior was born into the world.

Spirituality confronts "the Lie" that has plagued humankind throughout our history — we cannot find a solution to our problems outside of ourselves. Indeed if we look for solutions outside of ourselves we only create more problems. There is no obsession or compulsion that can take away the pain of being imperfect. There is no controlling behavior pattern or set of beliefs that will ever make us "as God." There is no escape from the moments of suffering that affects every human being at some time in their lives. Seeking such a fix can lead to obsessive-compulsive behavior.

Spirituality reminds us that we are *all* children of God. The compelling message in the first chapters of Genesis is important to hear today: *What God made is good.* Guilt, shame, judgments and self-pity are the tools that compulsive and obsessive behavior uses to beat us into slavery. And it seems to be working. To believe "The Lie" that human beings have no merit or divine power in their own right is to eventually live that lie.

I am reminded of a story that carries a warning, especially for the religious amongst us. A man visited a town where on every cross street was a church or mission hall. "My word," the stranger said, "These people must surely love God." "I truly hope so," said an old lady in a local shop, "because they sure do a good job of hating each other!"

We are all children of God. We have the spiritual power to create loving lives. The responsibility for recovery from compulsive and obsessive behavior is ours. God's miracle exists within each of us.

Father Leo Booth
1 (800) 284-2804

What We Have Discovered at OCA

We, as a fellowship, have found that together we can get well when separately we could not. Many of us have spent countless hours "battling" our obsessions and compulsions, swearing them off forever only to find ourselves right back where we started. *There is a solution!* The Twelve Steps, as originated by Alcoholics Anonymous, and adapted for OCA, can bring much relief to our common dilemma. Most of us have found that using this program along with our friends in the meetings can reduce or eliminate our obsessions and compulsions. We have found it most helpful in our meetings to emphasize the Twelve Steps and the program literature while discussing our personal stories since it is the program that brings the much desired relief. Discussions of a personal nature are encouraged but are used to reinforce how we apply the program in our lives today.

We have also found it useful to emphasize how we practiced the program today. Examples include calling our sponsor, helping another person with OCD, taking our inventory and praying to a Higher Power.* We have found this daily emphasis much more satisfying than dwelling on our obsessions and compulsions and whether we had a "good or bad day" with them. If we practice the program on a daily basis our obsessions and compulsions will take on less importance and our program will take root to grow and flourish, providing us relief.

It appears that meetings can provide a daily foundation for our recovery because it is there that we are reminded who we are and what the program suggests we

---

*To be further discussed in the chapter "The Recovery Program."

do to recover. There are a whole host of anonymous twelve step groups which welcome us with open arms. We suggest you call your local self-help clearinghouse to find out what program is available in your area if OCA is not nearby. Although these other 12-Step meetings may not specifically address OCD, you can still find the program and the fellowship and take this applied knowledge in starting a local OCA group. This will often reinforce your recovery even further.

Lastly, if you are not familar with what you find in this book, relax, you do not have to understand or apply it all at once. Gradually much of what is discussed here will begin to infiltrate your life and the desired changes will come. In the meantime read on and make meetings.

The Recovery Program

Our program of recovery is one that works. Here you will find the "Twelve Steps" which have been our key to a new life. Many of you will feel that this is too much to ask, that it won't work for you. We only ask that you give it a fraction of the time and energy you've put into perpetuating your OCD.

As we began to follow these suggestions our lives improved and our OCD lessened. Since ours is a program of action, actually *doing* what is outlined here seems to produce the results. With God's help we move away from our obsessive-compulsiveness and into a fellowship of recovering friends.

Here are the steps that outline our program:

Step 1. We admitted we were powerless over our obsessions and compulsions — that our lives had become unmanageable.

Step 2. Came to believe that a Power greater than ourselves could restore us to sanity.

Step 3. Made a decision to turn our will and our lives over to the care of God *as we understood Him.*

Step 4. Made a searching and fearless moral inventory of ourselves.

Step 5. Admitted to God, to ourselves, and to another human being the exact nature of our wrongs.

Step 6. Were entirely ready to have God remove all these defects of character.

Step 7. Humbly asked Him to remove our shortcomings.

Step 8. Made a list of all persons we had harmed, and became willing to make amends to them all.

Step 9. Made direct amends to such people wherever possible, except when to do so would injure them or others.

Step 10. Continued to take personal inventory and when we were wrong promptly admitted it.

Step 11. Sought through prayer and meditation to improve our conscious contact with God *as we understood Him,* praying only for knowledge of His will for us and the power to carry that out.

Step 12. Having had a spiritual awakening as the result of these steps, we tried to carry this message to those who still suffer from Obsessive Compulsive Disorder, and to practice these principles in all our affairs.*

The 12 Steps of A.A.

1. We admitted we were powerless over alcohol - that our lives had become unmanageable.
2. Came to believe that a Power greater than ourselves could restore us to sanity.
3. Made a decision to turn our will and our lives over to the care of God, AS WE UNDERSTOOD HIM.
4. Made a searching and fearless moral inventory of ourselves.
5. Admitted to God, to ourselves and to another human being the exact nature of our wrongs.
6. Were entirely ready to have God remove all these defects of character.
7. Humbly asked Him to remove our shortcomings.
8. Made a list of all persons we had harmed, and became willing to make amends to them all.

*A.A.'s Twelve Steps adapted with permission of A.A. World Services Inc.

9. Made direct amends to such people wherever possible, except when to do so would injure them or others.

10. Continued to take personal inventory and when we were wrong promptly admitted it.

11. Sought through prayer and meditation to improve our conscious contact with God AS WE UNDERSTOOD HIM, praying only for knowledge of His will for us and the power to carry that out.

12. Having had a spiritual awakening as the result of these steps, we tried to carry this message to alcoholics, and to practice these principles in all our affairs.

The Twelve Steps reprinted with permission of Alcoholics Anonymous World Services, Inc. The opinions expressed on this material are those of OCA only and not AA.

Step 1. *We admitted we were powerless over our obsessions and compulsions — that our lives had become unmanageable.* Obsessive Compulsive Disorder had us "licked". The harder we fought our obsessions and compulsions the harder they fought back. It is only by admitting that we were losing our lone battles against OCD that we can recover to enjoy a happy and fulfilling life.

When first presented with this concept, most of us were surprised. We came to OCA expecting to build up will power against OCD. Instead we learned that we were victims of obsessions and compulsions so strong that no amount of human will power could break them. As long as we continued our individual battles against OCD we would likely fall victim time and time again. Acceptance, on a gut level, that we cannot "negotiate" with our obsessions and compulsions is our admission of powerlessness.

Many of us could not admit that our lives had become unmanageable since we might have still had a good job, our families, a nice home, etc. We were then told that unmanageability didn't mean that we had to lose these things, although others of us did. The first step says that our lives had became unmanageable and for some of us not being able to enjoy our lives was unmanageable enough.

When we became ready to do *anything* to lift this merciless problem from us we were ready for the rest of this program.

Step 2. *Came to believe that a Power greater than ourselves could restore us to sanity.* This step asks us to believe in something which many of us feel we cannot. Some of us won't believe in a Higher Power, others can't. Still others who do believe in something have no faith whatsoever that a miracle will be performed on their behalf. Others felt that belief in a Higher Power was totally unscientific and just nonsense.

It appears that the *belief* in a power that could restore us to sanity is all that is needed. Many recovering from Obsessive Compulsive Disorders maintain that since they made an attempt to believe in a Higher Power they got results. The minute we stopped arguing and fighting this point, Step 2 gradually came to us.

To effect this approach, some of us have made our groups the "Higher Power" since they are certainly a power greater than just one lone individual suffering with OCD.

Those who lack faith often feel that God has turned His back on them. Organized religion was just another corporate enterprise; besides, prayer never helped anyway

OBSESSIVE COMPULSIVE ANONYMOUS

The answer has to do with the quality of faith rather than its quantity. The fact is we never applied the 12 Steps to clean up our side of the road so that the Grace of God could relieve our obsessions and compulsions. We never acknowledged our personality defects, made amends to those we hurt (including ourselves), or unselfishly tried to help another with OCD.

Whether agnostic, atheist, or believer, we can take the second step to the best of our ability right here and now.

Step 3. *Made a decision to turn our will and our lives over to the care of God as we understood Him.* At first glance Step 3 seemed impossible to many of us. Fortunately we can tell you that by just coming to a meeting or reading this book you have already begun this important step. All who have joined OCA and intend to try, have already begun to set aside their self-will to listen to another's ideas about Obsessive Compulsive Disorder.

The facts speak for themselves — the more we work for the willingness to depend upon a Power greater than ourselves the more independent and happy we become. Obviously our problems haven't been solved by will power since "playing God" hasn't worked well for us.

People with OCD are fortunate in the sense that we have suffered enough under our own rigid guidelines for life that we were driven to this program which allows us to look to a different source for guidance. Often we are victimized by remorse and guilt when we think of how OCD has affected our lives. Our lone courage and unaided will cannot bring us out of our lonely OCD prison.

Step 3 must be given a fair try since many of our troubles have been caused by the misuse of will power.

We have tried to bombard our problems with it instead of attempting to bring it into agreement with God's intention for us.[5] Our self-centered obsessive thoughts and compulsive behaviors have left us little room for those we care about. We could not change this frame of mind by wishing or trying on our own power. We had to have God's help.

The decision to turn our will and our lives over to the care of a Higher Power must be given a determined and persistent effort. Some of us have turned our will over in stages, maybe at first to the program and group of people in the program. We look for our Higher Power to express himself through others since God often works through people. This can often develop into the willingness to depend upon a Higher Power who is "running the show" for us. Acceptance of God's will for us leaves us free to enjoy life instead of fighting it all the time. We are no longer in "control" - we live life on life's terms. We still exert ourselves, though, applying the principles of this program to grow into our new way of life.

The Serenity Prayer can be used at any time we feel that we are losing our "God consciousness." We simply say, "God grant me the serenity to accept the things I cannot change, courage to change the things I can and the wisdom to know the difference." We reaffirm here that God's will, not ours, will be done.

Step 4. *Made a searching and fearless moral inventory of ourselves.* An inventory of our liabilities now will free up our lives later. Many of us did not realize that we were carrying so much "emotional baggage" until we thoroughly did this step. Some of us also felt that we

---

[5] Twelve Steps and Twelve Traditions (New York: A.A. World Services Inc. 1981), p.40.

really were defect-free except for our obsessive and compulsive behaviors. Still others said that their present anxieties and troubles were caused by the behavior of other people who should change their ways.

Step 4 is a comprehensive effort to reveal the defects of character that are hurting ourselves and others. We clean up only *our* side of the road and do not look for the wrongs done by others.

Many of us have felt that a written list of resentments was a good place to start since resentments hurt us more than we know.

A suggested approach:

I'm resentful at: (People, Institutions, or principles)	The Cause (Why we were angry)	Affects my:
Mr. Doe	Unreasonable boss Doesn't appreciate my abilities	May lose job Self esteem (fear)
Myself	Obsessive compulsive behavior	Self-esteem (fear)
My spouse	Opinionated Domineering	Pride Sex relations

This list of resentments and their effects allows us to crystallize their impact on our lives.

Others have found their defects in the "seven deadly sins" of pride, greed, lust, anger, gluttony, envy and sloth. Those full of pride will often feel that they don't need to look any further, that all their problems are caused by factors outside themselves. Others may feel that they have a right to be angry since the world hasn't been kind to them and that people have wronged them. Still some feel they have to grab for more of everything and when disappointed, take out their frustration on others. The simple fact for us is that holding onto these defects of character makes us sick. This is also true if we are justified in having these feelings. Anger and resentment shut us out from spiritual growth and move us back into our destructive pattern. We simply cannot afford to harbor these feelings if we want to recover.

Fear often touches every aspect of our lives. By reviewing our fears thoroughly and putting them on paper we expose them for what they are. We use the same chart as we did for our resentments listing also the cause and effect of our fears. We meet these fears with faith once we look to a Higher Power and the fellowship for guidance.

Sex is sometimes very troublesome but can be dealt with as any other life situation. We look for anger, resentments, jealousy and envy and ask for guidance. We list those whom we hurt with our sex conduct, what we did, and how it ultimately affected us. We also must not forget those times we used sex as a weapon, perhaps by withholding it from our mates or flirting outside our relationship. We often find that honestly asking ourselves, "Did I act selfishly?" can serve as a guiding direction.

We can end our inventory by looking at our relationships with family and friends. Here we often find ourselves dominating these people, or to the other extreme, leaning on them too heavily. This self-centered behavior can only add to our problems. We must form a partnership with people and look at how we can help them rather than what they should be doing for us.

We hope that the reader will examine this step closely since our defects are often buried under layers of self-justification. We take this step to the best of our ability now knowing that this is the beginning of a lifelong process with Step 10.

Step 5. *Admitted to God, to ourselves, and to another human being the exact nature of our wrongs.* Here we are given the opportunity to dump all the garbage we have been carrying around since it is this load that increases our obsessive-compulsive behavior. We know from a personal vantage point that we tended to be secretive about our OCD because we felt it was embarrassing, personal, or that people just wouldn't understand. But upon closer inspection we sometimes found that we kept this problem a secret because we didn't want anyone to interfere with our little rituals or obsessions; *we simply would deal with them on our own.* Here in Step 5 we find that opening communication with God and another human being lifts this burden of secrecy from us. We soon get used to the idea that God knows all about us after all.

But it is when we are honest with another person that it confirms we have been honest with ourselves and with God. We share our inventory with someone whose only real job is to listen and offer advice as needed. Here we turn back to Step 4 where we focused in on our defects of character. We experience humility by confiding these defects with a trusted individual. This may be another member of the group, a close friend, therapist, clergyperson or sponsor. We also learn where we might have exaggerated or dramatized our shortcomings. We find where our stock-taking has been productive, and learn from this "housecleaning."

At this point many of us have experienced great relief by emerging from the isolation our obsessive-compulsiveness has imposed on us. Our burden of guilt and shame is no longer ours to bear alone. The focus begins to move away from our personal concerns into the stream of life once we let God and someone else into our world.

Step 6. *Were entirely ready to have God remove all these defects of character.* This step appears to be something we would like to do. Who would want to hang on to his defects of character? But experience shows that most of us are only willing to let go of some of these defects while holding on tightly to others. We are perhaps "comfortable" with some of our old attitudes and ways or maybe we just don't know how we can live without our own rigid guidelines. We can tell you that as God removes our defects of character we are freed from the self-imposed prison that Obsessive Compulsive Disorder wraps us in.

Here we do not expect the immediate removal of our defects. Patient improvement is what we strive for and in God's time much of what is objectionable will be lifted.

Let us examine some of our defects more closely now. Perfectionism is one we seem to see a lot of. By trying to make things "perfect" (which is impossible) we destroy our chances for a happy life. Our repeated attempts to make things "perfect" only bring on anxiety and stress which in turn fuel this fire. We must look to a Higher Power and the program for guidance in this matter since self-knowledge doesn't work. *Acceptance* can replace our perfectionistic tendencies when we "let go" of our control.

Self-righteous anger can be a very dangerous defect of character. We sometimes take satisfaction with anger because of how someone has wronged us. We may blame other people for our problems because of things they said or did. Even if we have a "right" to be angry we cannot stay so for long if we hope for spiritual growth.

Self-pity seems to be a common character defect we share. For some reason we look to "whine" about our state of affairs, feeling sorry for ourselves and crying in our cups. Many of us feel that we have been dealt an unfair hand in the game of life and if only *all* of our OCD and other problems would go away we would be happy. Through our program we come to accept that although things in our lives might be better, we really are *not* bearing the weight of the world. *Everyone* has their own problems and OCD just happens to be ours. We don't believe we were responsible for getting OCD, but now that we have it we need to work a recovery program for it. We have found it helpful when we start to feel sorry for ourselves to put energy instead into helping another member of OCA.

"Control" seems to be a problematic area for most of us. Our obsessive-compulsive nature looks to control our environment and thoughts in a way that is excessive and self-destructive. On the other hand we often find ourselves dominated by other people who "control" us. We instead need to set clear boundaries between others and ourselves so that our personal freedoms and desires can be expressed. By declaring our emotional independence from controlling individuals we are further freed from our obsessive-compulsiveness.

This action may take courage and patience but the end result is change and personal integrity. We no longer fall back on our control games with others - we have the option of leaving any personal rut we find ourselves in. We need no longer be trapped in controlling families, jobs or relations. Action and change go hand in hand with our recovery from OCD.

Another defect of character we seem to share involves our *inability to change* the things that are clearly hurting us. A prime example is seen in our self-destructive relationships with certain people. These relationships may be found in our jobs, families and friendships. As we work our program of recovery we look for guidance concerning these personal matters. *We don't have to stay with people who pull us down into our obsessive-compulsive ways.* We look for the courage to sever these relationships which we originally thought we couldn't function without. Of course there will be situations in which repairing the relationship is also an option - but we must be ready to put our recovery from OCD first. This may mean making a swift clean break from a truly destructive dependency on another, however painful that may be.

Many of us also share the defect of blaming our Obsessive Compulsive Disorder and ourselves for the situations we have gotten into. This is really just our pride and ego in reverse-negative pride. It seems that we either build ourselves up to heights which we cannot attain or cut ourselves down by character assassination. *Acceptance of self right where we are NOW puts us on the road to recovery.*

This program allows us to progress toward the goal of readiness to part with our defects of character. We continue to work with this objective in Step 7, moving towards God's will for us.

Step 7. *Humbly asked Him to remove our shortcomings.* Without humility our chances of recovery are greatly lessened. We saw earlier that we were indeed powerless over our obsessions and compulsions and that a power greater than ourselves could restore us to sanity. It was by admitting defeat and turning to a strength outside ourselves that we were able to initiate recovery. Here in this step we begin to become convinced that living on our own individual strength and intelligence alone makes a working faith in a Higher Power impossible.

It appears that the chief activator of our obsessive-compulsiveness has been self-centered fear — primarily fear that we would lose something we already possessed or would fail to get something we demanded. Living upon a basis of unsatisfied demands we were in a state of continual disturbance and frustration.[6] We were constantly demanding things to be just the way we wanted them to be instead of aligning our will with that of God's.

It seems among us that we've often placed material achievements and external comforts above character building and spiritual values. We do not wish to minimize material achievement and success, but we can tell you from experience that living solely along these lines drives us back into our obsessive-compulsiveness. With humility as our guide, we move away from these "externals" in our world toward helping our fellow man and improving our relationship with our Higher Power.

For us this new outlook comes only after repeated sufferings with our own self-destructive attitudes and behaviors. In our fellowship we have seen how the misery of OCD is transformed by humility into something positive. We hear story after story of how humility has brought *strength* out of weakness. Our character defects have led us into making unreasonable demands upon ourselves, others and God. We are now willing to apply humility toward removing our shortcomings so that we may be of better service to those around us. Most of us have found that our shortcomings which fire our obsessive-compulsiveness are gradually removed in God's time.

[6] *Twelve Steps and Twelve Traditions* (New York: A.A. World Services, Inc. 1981), p. 76.

Step 8. *Made a list of all persons we had harmed, and became willing to make amends to them all.* Here we look for the willingness to face those we have hurt to best repair the damage done. We actually have made a beginning with our moral inventory in Step 4. We turn to our charts of resentment, fear and sex conduct to find the people we have harmed.

When looking at a troubled relationship, we often go on the defensive. We may only want to look at how we've been hurt instead of the total picture. Often we have strained the relationship to bring out the worst in others. Some of us, still troubled with denial, cling to the proposition that our OCD never hurt anybody but ourselves. Certainly we hurt ourselves, but we must not forget the suffering we inflicted on those who cared for us the most. They *also* were the victims of our obsessions and compulsions. We do not wish to enter into a debate over whether we were responsible for the suffering our obsessive-compulsive personalities inflicted but we *do know* that we hurt others and to recover we must be willing to make amends.

Many of us have found that our obsessive-compulsiveness has harmed others on levels previously unexplored. Some subtler ways we emotionally and spiritually have hurt people may be seen in our family lives. We may happen to be inflexible, callous, critical, impatient, humorless, or wallow in self-pity, or lash out at others. We may also bring these attitudes into our day-to-day affairs, making life harder for all about us. We now use this new-found outlook to find those people who have been negatively affected, meanwhile forgiving the wrongs done us. We are looking for the willingness to forgive ourselves and others for the rough spots in our personal relationships. The willingness to make amends can free us from our resentments which ultimately frees us from our obsessive-compulsiveness.

There might be some instances where restitution is impossible. Examples include people who have died, those who won't agree to talk with us, or amends better deferred for other reasons. This doesn't excuse us from an accurate survey of our past life as it has affected other people. In taking this step we should avoid extreme judgments of both ourselves and others and be most careful not to exaggerate our task at hand.

Step 9. *Made direct amends to such people wherever possible, except when to do so would injure them or others.* In this step, we find our sea of resentments "washing clean." It is here that we meet with those on our list and attempt to repair the damage done, freeing us into "emotional sobriety."

The people we make amends to will often be receptive to our approach, even if we hurt them beyond repair. But it seems we often find that many of our conflicts have been one sided with only us holding onto anger. We seem to be of the temperament to hold a grudge long beyond the average fellow's forgetting of the same. Here we are allowed to forgive both others and ourselves for those stored emotions which have hurt us so.

There will also be certain amends which are not so benign. Obviously, if we have cheated someone in some way, we should rectify the problem as soon as possible. Our self-centeredness can easily compromise our natural tendencies to be honest and fair. It is most important in the amends process that we do not *increase* the harm we have already done. Examples include revealing names in a detailed account of an extra-marital affair when your spouse suspects nothing. Or perhaps we have padded an expense account which our associates little suspect. Here we must look carefully with the guidance of a Higher Power and those in the program to decide how these situations must be handled. What we are trying to do is heal these problems, not throw salt on the wound. We must be certain not to injure others or ourselves further, but we must be willing to make amends as fast and as far as we possibly can.

It seems appropriate here to mention self-forgiving in the amends process. We have often been our own worst enemies regarding our obsessive-compulsiveness. Here we can forgive ourselves and accept that we are OK where we are now.

If we are serious about working on our recovery we will feel amazing results before we are halfway done. We will taste a new freedom from our obsessive-compulsiveness. We will accept our past and grow from it. We will feel peace of mind that we never thought possible. We will realize that our experience can now help others. Self-pity and shame will leave us. Our self-centeredness will be replaced with a trust in others and God. Our negative attitudes and behaviors will decrease. Our insecurities and fears concerning people will lessen. We will now welcome change instead of fear it. Our priorities and concerns will move away from ourselves and into helping others. Self-hate will be replaced with self-esteem. Life will no longer be a constant struggle with no relief in sight. We will feel God working in our lives today.

Are these exaggerated promises? We know they are not. They are happening for us. If we work for them they will always materialize in time.

Step 10. *Continued to take personal inventory and when we were wrong promptly admitted it.* A continuous look at our liabilities (as well as assets) seems to be necessary for us. We need to survey our attitudes during the day, watching for anger, resentment, fear, inflexibility and self-centered thinking. Daily we cast up a balance sheet and semi-annually we go in for a total housecleaning. Many of us felt that these practices were too time consuming and really didn't apply. We found out instead that these few minutes spent in self-examination saved us hours of suffering with our obsessions and compulsions. Making this practice a daily part of our lives makes us happier and allows us to be more kind and tolerant towards others.

A spot-check inventory can be taken during the day anytime we are disturbed by anger, self-pity, resentments or a host of other character defects we have previously identified. In these situations in our lives we need to look for self-restraint and a willingness to admit when the fault is ours. We should avoid speaking or acting hastily which can damage our relationships with others. We must avoid argument and criticism with others, as well as silent anger.

We can try to stop making unreasonable demands upon those we love, including ourselves. We can show unselfishness towards those we've frequently ignored. It will become more and more evident in time that it is senseless to become angry or to get hurt by people who are also living in this sometimes difficult world of ours. In this continuous look at our inventory we strive for progress, not perfection.

When evening comes many of us draw up a balance sheet for the day. Credit and Debit are present on this paper since we often do constructive things during our day despite our character defects. We look for *motives* in our thoughts or acts since our motives will determine if we were selfish or not. We sometimes find ourselves hiding a bad intention underneath a veil of good. We needlessly argued with someone because *we* were full of fear and anger or we complained about our state of affairs seeking only attention and sympathy. "If only people would see it our way," we wailed. This veil of self-righteousness has to be lifted if we hope to change.

Putting this step to daily use with the help of our friends in the program will allow us to spot more quickly the defects of character which drag us down into our obsessive compulsiveness. If we have an honest regret for harms done and a willingness to try for better tomorrows we will grow away from our problems and into God's solution for us.

Step 11. *Sought through prayer and meditation to improve our conscious contact with God as we understood Him, praying only for knowledge of His will for us and the power to carry that out.* Prayer and meditation can work for us even if our beliefs lean toward those of the agnostic or atheist. There is a direct linkage among self-examination, meditation and prayer. Taken separately these practices can bring much relief and benefit. But when they are logically related and interwoven the result is an unshakable foundation for life.[7]

Simply experimenting with prayer and meditation can lead to unexplained results. Some of us have found that applying the concept of "just for today" we pray today - not committing ourselves to a lifetime of recitals.

---

[7] *Twelve Steps and Twelve Traditions* (New York: A.A. World Services, Inc. 1981) p. 98.

This approach allows us to resume prayer if we find that this part of our program has fallen by the wayside.

Many of us have found that beginning and ending our day with prayer has given us a new strength. We can find many wonderful prayers from an infinite number of sources. Our sponsors or spiritual advisors can guide us to them. When meditating we listen for direction from our Higher Power looking for knowledge of His will for us. Upon awakening we recall that our well being is dependent on our relationship with our Higher Power through the program.

When we pray we must be careful not to ask for specific things because we don't know if what we are praying for is in accord with God's will. We *do* know that God loves us and wants us to be happy and that this happiness can be found by aligning our will with that of God's. As the day goes on we pause where situations must be met and renew the simple request, "Thy will, not mine, be done."

God may not always answer our prayers in the manner in which we might expect Him. God speaks through many mediums, of which we may be aware of only a few. We have found that decision making is more fruitful if we make use of this program and the people in it for guidance and support on any matters we may be facing. We don't *have* to be alone anymore. The world may not seem so hostile now; we are no longer lost, frightened and purposeless. Prayer and meditation have brought our Higher Power into our day-to-day affairs.

Step 12. *Having had a spiritual awakening as the result of these steps, we tried to carry this message to those who still suffer from*

Obsessive Compulsive Disorder, and to practice these principles in all our affairs. Here we are given a chance to bring the message of recovery to those who still live in the lonely prison of OCD. This vital step is done enthusiastically without thought of reward or praise. *Our* stage of OCD recovery is unimportant. We can still spread this program even if we are the newest of new or if we have had a relapse.

Here we must also talk about the "spiritual awakening" as a result of taking the previous eleven steps. Thankfully, this doesn't mean we have all experienced a sudden profound uplifting. More often a gradual rearrangement of our attitudes and priorities results in a new state of consciousness which we previously thought impossible. We have plugged ourselves into a source of strength which affords us peace of mind, unselfishness, tolerance and love. We are able to do, feel and believe things which we couldn't on our own.

Since OCD often has isolated us from the rest of the world, the twelfth step brings us out of our self-imposed prison. When carrying this message to others, we interact with people like us who uniquely understand. No longer are our obsessions and compulsions ours to bear alone. We have a fellowship which will come through for us if we are willing to get out of ourselves to help and be helped by others.

When meeting someone who might be interested in our program we have found it best to stick to our own stories. We are not in a position to preach or educate. Our experience is our best advocate. There will be those who might reject this approach citing that it isn't scientific or doesn't apply to them. Don't argue this point, just explain what OCA has done for you. Working with others is the foundation of our recovery. A kind act or an occasional phone call won't cut it. We must let others into our lives in order to recover, lest we go back to our old painful, destructive ways.

We have also found that those of us who are receiving medical or psychological help for their OCD can also work this program with good results. We, as a fellowship, take no position on specific outside treatments. We do know that this program has helped us tremendously.

Practicing these principles in all of our affairs simply asks us to take our program with us in whatever situation we may find ourselves. Many of us have noticed that if we practice program daily, we find ourselves watching our resentments and anger, forgiving others of their mistakes and in general a greater tolerance and acceptance of life just the way it is. Our demands for the world to be just the way *we* want it to be will lessen. We may start, instead, to think how we can make someone else's day easier instead of how difficult our own lives can be.

Before program, many of us saw our OCD aggravated by situations around us or problems we may have had. So in response, we tried to arrange these situations to our satisfaction, hoping that this change in our external world would help our OCD. Through OCA we came to realize that the changes must instead come from within. We also saw that we had to think of others outside of ourselves, especially those still suffering from OCD. We try to carry the "OCA spirit" into our daily work, our personal relations, and our relationship with our Higher Power. We, who have struggled alone for so long with OCD, have found that in trying to help others, our personal struggles with OCD take on less importance. This is the paradox we have found. The solution lies *outside* of ourselves and rests with the willingness to help and be helped by others and our Higher Power.

Another benefit we have found by bringing program into our day-to-day affairs is the change we have had in our relationship with others. Previously we have found ourselves overly dependent on people as a sick child on his parent or to the other extreme, welcoming no one's help or opinions into our lives, living exclusively by our own rigid guidelines. Often we lived in shame, isolating ourselves from others and thinking that no one could possibly understand. Instead, we need to form a partnership with others. When we strive to be open to suggestion and trust our fellow man, years of negative relations with others can melt away. We find this applicable in all aspects of our lives, including job, family and friends.

We bring this presentation of the Twelve Steps to a close here. This program is not a theory, we have to live it if we want recovery in our lives. Progress is what we strive for and in time our obsessive-compulsiveness will be relieved if we keep coming back to give this way of life a chance to work for us.

We Can Do Together...

I have been a member of OCA for almost a year, and I am also a member of another twelve-step group. In my other group, we do a lot of socializing — we go out on weekends for beach parties, picnics, etc. I thought, "Wouldn't it be nice to do that with my OCA group, too?" Then I started thinking about all of the reasons why I thought it could never work out for us. Just imagine it — the "checkers" would never get there on time . . . lots of us afraid to drive (we might hit cars or people — and then we might not know for sure if we'd done it...) ...some of us don't like to collect money (afraid we might steal it accidentally, or become contaminated from handling it) . . . and the people with contamination fears might worry about eating food prepared by the rest of us . . ." it would be a disaster!," I thought. At that point I began to feel even more isolated and sorry for myself . . .

Then I remembered my experience as a "shabbas goy." When I worked in campus ministry years ago, I became friends with the campus rabbi. We shared our traditions, and one day he asked me to be his "shabbas goy." Literally, this means "sabbath gentile," and it's a non-Jew who can help out a Jew in special circumstances when the Jew is unable to do something because of Jewish law. For example, a shabbas goy might turn on the lights or write something down for a Jewish friend on the sabbath day when orthodox Jews aren't permitted to do anything that constitutes "work". Or, my rabbi friend asked me to help him for one holy week when he was supposed to surrender all his possessions. He sold me everything he owned for a dollar for the week. I was flattered that he would share his traditions with me, and honored that he would trust me with all his worldly possessions (and knew that I would willingly sell them all back to him the next week for the same price!).

We at OCA do the same thing. Unlike orthodox Jews, who choose, as a community, to follow one set of laws, we in OCA each seem to suffer under a set of rigid and often tyrannical personal "laws" which bind us. Our personal laws are often shared by few others we know, if any. But we do have different laws, and in OCA we share a common understanding that enables us to transcend our differences (and sometimes even the laws themselves!) So maybe we can't all get to the beach or a picnic on time, or handle money, or feel comfortable driving, or cooking, but each one of us can do something; and we can actually admit to each other what we cannot do. So we COULD have a picnic, and actually be honest with each other. Imagine a social event where we would not have to lie (about why we were late, or why we don't want to participate in something), or avoid things, or disappear at certain uncomfortable times for us — a social event we don't avoid altogether because of our OCD! A social event where we could be ourselves? What a picnic that would be! I think we can do it. Together.

(1)
Once Was Never Enough

I've heard in the meetings that some people "acquire" Obsessive Compulsive Disorder (OCD). It seems that I was just born with it. I remember that during my childhood I arranged my toys in a particular pattern — not to be disturbed by anyone.

Perfectionism, an impossible goal, became my goal. In school, I managed to excel since I always completed my assignments before their due dates. My studies assumed an important part of my life which is why I finished college with the highest of honors and graduated professional school to enter into my chosen field.

During those years, the main manifestations of my OCD were checking, counting and fear of dirt and contamination. Somehow I managed to keep it "under control" because I was so busy with my studies. I figured that this "quirk" in my personality enabled me to excel in school since I was able to "plan my life" better than most people.

I little realized how my OCD would turn on me. During those college years, I developed the acne problem common to adolescence. This normal condition turned into something very abnormal for me. I would spend countless hours picking at my skin until it bled. Mirrors assumed an important role in my life — almost every spare moment found me in front of one.

All personal efforts to stop failed. Removing the mirrors from the walls or disconnecting the lights became easily reversible. I found myself picking late into the evening despite the protests of my family. This ritual became my master; no human could stop me.

This intensified for about five years during which I sought professional help. Therapy produced no results for me. Hypnosis, biofeedback and a nutritionist were ineffective. Although my OCD was assuming a more important role in my life, I somehow managed to keep my job and my family. Those closest to me stuck by me no matter how hopeless the problem appeared to be while I, on the other hand, became very angry and sarcastic. I would often argue with people needlessly, defending my right to continue this behavior since my OCD seemed to be bothering them more than it was bothering me — so I claimed. My denial was firmly embedded. I didn't want anyone to interfere with my OCD rituals. I didn't realize that I had an illness that I could not recover from alone, that I needed an outside source of strength.

My turning point came when someone who knew me well mentioned that my problem reminded him very much of an addiction, particularly alcoholism. At first I resisted this concept but gradually, after reading some of Alcoholics Anonymous' literature, I became convinced of the similarity. Both OCD and alcoholism are addictive, out-of-control, misguided searches for feelings of relief which only result in pain.

By attending A.A. meetings, I began to get some relief. However, I didn't do what the program suggested, including practicing the 12 Steps, sponsorship, phone calls. I guess I wasn't really ready to commit myself to something that might actually work. I still thought that I could handle this problem on my own.

Around the Fall of 1987 news of Obsessive Compulsive Disorder became a media event. People just like me were on T.V. and in the newspapers. OCD was becoming a household word. I really thought that by now a group of us would have gotten together to try to help each other. I was hoping for the creation of a group that based its recovery on the same 12 Steps that numerous other anonymous programs successfully use. Sadly, this was not the case. How could this be? Obviously, since this approach was helping me, it had to help others.

January 1988 saw the beginning of Obsessive Compulsive Anonymous (OCA). I thought I would be the last person interested in starting a group like this. I was too "busy" with my work and family. Besides, I needed the extra time to perpetuate my OCD.

Reluctantly, I saw my course. Either I work the program to the best of my ability or fall back into my old patterns. Obsessive Compulsive Anonymous allowed me to participate fully in the 12 Step way of life. I came to believe that my recovery was dependent on a Higher Power and that I could do His work by working with others with OCD who want the program.

OCA has brightened my life beyond my expectations. I am no longer a daily victim of my OCD. My episodes are far apart and less intense. I no longer feel like I'm on the edge in constant turmoil. I actually can enjoy peace of mind. The people whom I thought I had to change no longer need changing; they are who they are. I don't feel trapped by people, places or things. I have options today. I participate in life — I'm no longer a victim of it. I look forward to my meetings today because I have a chance to share with those who uniquely understand and will not criticize or judge me. I am also privileged to watch the newcomers who see that this is available to them, too, if they are willing to give the program half the time and energy that they gave their OCD. As long as the Higher Power requires my participation in OCA, I will gratefully pass on the gift which has been given to me.

Postscript

Since first writing this story, things in my life have changed even more. Recovery from OCD has proven challenging since experiencing life has proven more real than hiding in my rituals.

My relations with other people (especially my spouse) were strained in early recovery. I guess that when two people have spent years of their lives trying to control the OCD, they then find themselves left with just each other once the disease is no longer the central theme of their existence together. Therefore, adjustments must be made. I've spoken with many people in OCA who have gone through such "adjustments" and I'm glad that I'm not alone.

Recently, I've also had to face the biological realities associated with OCD. My four-year-old daughter had an "acute" OCD episode. I can only describe this experience as terrifying. Seeing the manifestations of this illness in someone so young and so close to me has been extremely painful. I know, though, that this program and knowledgeable professionals are there for her with insight and help that wasn't available to me when I was her age.

As a result, her recovery is nothing short of remarkable. She has recently been able to face her worst fears and walk through them. Most importantly, my wife and I have reset our priorities as parents. We have come to realize that a child's freedom to make mistakes is more important than getting a stain on a new dress or skinning a knee from running too fast. The *last* thing that a child with OC tendencies needs is to feel that she or he has to be "perfect."

As a parent recovering from OCD, my innate tendency to overprotect her has been replaced with looser guidelines and letting go of my control. Since *I* see the world as a safer place, now she can also interpret *her* world that way. Her mistakes are now treated as experiences to learn from instead of only things necessary to correct. Introducing the concept of a loving God to our child has allowed her to experience the unconditional love we feel for her regardless of her shortcomings. We've allowed her to recognize that God loves us all, even when we mess up.

I feel that it is also important to mention the changes that I've experienced in my relationships with other people as my recovery continues. By working diligently, my wife and I have been able to renew our closeness which was torn by the OCD. Things are better between us now than they have ever been. My parents and I have been able to forgive each other and the special feelings that I had for them as a child are returning.

I am fortunate that working the Twelve-Step program of OCA has dramatically reduced my OCD. Because it is such a vicious disease, I was willing to do *anything* (including starting OCA) to get relief from it.

To further my recovery, I've recently begun taking medication commonly used for OCD. I feel that *my* recovery in the Twelve-Step program can be enhanced by availing myself of all the possible avenues of relief from OCD.

I am grateful for what OCA has done for me and with God's help, others can find the relief that I've been privileged to enjoy.

(2)
Sobriety From OCD

I think I've been putting off writing my story for so long because I just don't want to remember the pain I went through with the OCD. I'm experiencing such good recovery that I almost don't want to remember the pain, but I know that by writing this story and having it appear in this book I might help others to recover and maybe someone out there can identify with what I've gone through.

I had a rough childhood. My father was a very abusive alcoholic, emotionally and sometimes physically. I was always a nervous, frightened child who felt different from everyone else. I also felt that there was something wrong with me. I probably suffered from OCD as far back as I can remember. I became obsessed with different things, but I was mostly obsessed with my appearance and my bodily functions, odors and other things like that. I can also remember having an obsession with the curse word "shit" which got really bad as time went on. When I was a child my mother literally washed my mouth out with soap for saying that word. I can't say for sure if that was definitely related to my obsession, but as I think back, I realize that it probably was; it doesn't take a psychiatrist to figure that one out.

That obsession probably lasted for a good year and it was torture. I was always afraid that I was going to blurt it out or that someone knew that I was thinking that word and I would get banished to hell or something like that, for having that word in my mind. It produced a lot of panic attacks, isolation and fear. Somehow, I barely made it through high school. I graduated, got married and got a job, but was always nervous and fearful.

My main obsession, though, was with my facial expression. I focused mostly on my eyes and was extremely self-conscious. I believed that they looked bizarre and that one eye was larger than the other. I checked them in the mirror hundreds of times a day to see if they actually looked as bizarre as I thought they did. Of course, I believed that they looked a certain way and was convinced of that. Then, as the years passed, the job I worked at for about ten years was coming to an end because the company was merging with a larger company. Since I don't take well to change, I became very frightened. I think that people with OCD are almost allergic to change, whether it's positive or negative change.

Until that point my OCD consisted primarily of obsessional thoughts. I started to compulsively stare at the ground or roll my eyes in my head, cross my eyes or even make distorted faces at people. It went hand in hand with the eyes and the facial expressions. I actually had conversations with people (which I desperately tried to avoid) in which I could barely concentrate on what they were saying to me. Instead, during the conversation, I was thinking about what my face looked like. This caused me a lot of anxiety, fear, and self-hatred as well as embarrassment. This just seemed too idiotic to me, and yet I couldn't stop. The more I tried to control it and relax my face, the worse it became. I bought every self-help book imaginable, I tried psychotherapy and I was in a hospital for a month. At the age of 16 I was prescribed medication for severe migraine headaches. I believe that these headaches were actually the result of the stress in my home caused by my father's alcoholism and the anxiety that I felt from OCD. I also tried bio-feedback and hypnosis. I tried everything from diets to exercise programs to combat this OCD. Some things helped me temporarily but it always seemed that the OCD would come back even stronger and worse than it was before. Whenever the OCD seemed to be somewhat in remission, it would inevitably come back even harder.

Somehow I gave birth to two daughters, 18 months apart. After the birth of my second child I began developing an obsession with the untrue notion that I was yelling out obscenities and didn't hear myself.

I was so withdrawn and into my own little world that the only time I left my home was when I had to go food shopping or take care of other necessities. I even wore sunglasses so that no one would see my eyes. I was a mess. The OCD had gotten so bad that I was afraid that if I left my home and I was out yelling obscenities, which I never was, I would be locked up and my kids would be taken away. I had all of these horrible fears. When I shopped, I clung to the shopping cart for dear life with my sweaty palms, ready to break the cart in half. I just wanted to get this trauma over with and go home in the security of my house.

The OCD seemed to hit me harder when I was outside of my home. In my house I had a feeling of safety, but when I was around other people it was really difficult to function.

I also had other obsessive behaviors with house-cleaning. I was always either up on a ladder scrubbing down walls, or mopping the floors. I also became very obsessed with my children. When they played I didn't like having toys about and I liked everything tidied up. I was just like a patrol person around my home. No one could relax or live comfortably in this home. I just patrolled around all the time picking up lint from the floor or cleaning up toys that my kids wanted to play with. They weren't allowed to have them out because I got upset when things were out of order. For a while the obsession with the eyes and the compulsion to make faces got very bad. I couldn't look at a person without doing something strange with my face or my eyes. Often, I was staring so intently at the floor that it looked as though I was going to collapse. I tortured myself afterward and felt such self-hatred. Thinking back, I believe that the OCD got so bad that I was losing sleep at night. I did what they caution a person against in AA. I didn't HALT and I got too Hungry, Angry, Lonely and Tired. I was always very tired because I was nursing my youngest daughter and my sleep was broken up by the feedings. I was walking around like a zombie with these fears and compulsions.

I finally hit rock bottom about three years ago. Everything had gotten so bad that I remember sitting in the corner of my bedroom thinking about killing myself. I was seriously contemplating suicide because I couldn't live the way I was living another day.

I felt that I was an awful mother because I just wasn't there for my kids. I started scolding my oldest daughter and found myself always angry at her. I knew it was my self-hatred projected onto this child and I felt that I was the worst mother in the world. I felt that I was insane and that there was something wrong with my brain. I believed that I would really be doing everyone a favor by just killing myself.

I was a very angry person with no belief in God or any Higher Power. I was hateful toward everybody and I had no friends. While reading the newspaper one afternoon a few days after that night I came across an announcement for the 12-step program of Recoveries Anonymous. They used the word "obsessions" and referred to suffering with these obsessions or any other self-destructive behavior. I called and spoke to a woman who later became my sponsor.

I began going to meetings once a week but I went in there like I went into so many other things that I had tried. I was very skeptical, especially when they talked about a Higher Power or God. I thought spirituality meant religion. I was very, very leery but this woman said to me, "What do you have to lose? You've tried everything else. Just give it a fair shot and then decide." So, I thought to myself, . . . "I'll try this. This is my last straw. If this doesn't work, I will kill myself and then I will have known I tried everything."

So I started going to meetings, although in the beginning I refused to read the book *Alcoholics Anonymous*. I thought it was ridiculous and that my father should have read this book, but not me. I did not have an alcohol problem. I thought that for a while until little by little I could hear that my personality was that of an alcoholic.

I just did not click onto alcohol as my obsession. I started reading the book and just kept going to meetings. The woman who I had spoken to over the telephone became my sponsor. I went to a workshop to learn more about the 12 steps and I started to think, "Well, you know, there is something to this." I wrote my resentment list and realized that everybody and anybody that I had ever known was on that list. I wondered if it could be all these people or if it could be me. Could all of these people be so bad? I realized that there were a lot of things that I did to others that made them treat me in certain ways. There were also a lot of things in my past that I really had to look at and examine.

My actions were not the best, so I started to make amends to people that I had harmed. I began to take an inventory every day. I also started praying every night to my Higher Power, who I defined as Nature. I feel that I really connect with Nature as a power greater than myself that I can tap into. I didn't try to analyze the Program.

When I asked a lot of questions, the people in the rooms told me, "Try not overanalyze. Just try to work the steps to the best of your ability, and try to take it a day at a time." I started to meditate and I read a lot of other books that were suggested by another fellowship. I read the book entitled *Sermon on the Mount* which I really related to. It just seemed to make so much sense to me. I believe that after I finished reading that book I had a spiritual awakening of sorts and it was the turning point for me.

Also, after I had made some amends I began experiencing a peace of mind and serenity in my life that I had never known before. Anyone with OCD knows that feeling of the mind being on overdrive and not concentrating on anything. There is no peace in that state; it's constant. I was even dreaming the OCD.

I started to get periods of peace of mind. When I first joined the Program I said the serenity prayer over and over again. That seemed to help me a great deal. I remember writing it out and keeping it on a little card in my car and on my refrigerator. This really helped me. I started experiencing the OCD lifting and I began to have friends, which I had never had years ago. Back then I couldn't handle having anyone in my home. It was just too stressful and disruptive and caused me too much anxiety.

I met some really great people through the Program and I started to allow them into my home. I realized little by little that nothing terrible would happen. There is also a section with the promises in the "Big Book" that says that "fear of people will leave us." I had a big star next to that line because fear of people was a really big issue for me. This fear was starting to lift though and I was now able to have a conversation with a person without that self-consciousness and constant thinking about myself.

I started experiencing recovery and I knew that this was the answer for me. I just knew it; there was definitely something to this that wasn't like all those other things I had tried. This program was the answer. It was freedom and sanity. This was what I knew in my heart would be the answer for me.

Through Recoveries Anonymous I met OCA's founder. He called me one night and said that he was starting another fellowship called OCA and that he knew a little bit about my symptoms and my disease. At that time though there wasn't much talk about OCD. It wasn't "labeled."

I started going to two meetings per week and I think that was another turning point for me. It seemed like doubling up on the meetings really sped up my recovery process. I recommend to people that join these programs to try to get to more than one meeting a week; to try to get to as many meetings as possible, especially in the beginning when they're really suffering.

Then OCA started to develop and we began to realize that there are so many people with OCD. Suddenly, all of this information about the disease started becoming publicized. It feels so wonderful that this book is now being written and that people can come out of the closet about their OCD since the nature of this illness is to want to hide it because you feel like such a freak and that you're insane.

Now I'm meeting such wonderful people — all types of people. Our groups consist of doctors, teachers and all sorts of people that one would think just wouldn't have problems like this. They're really normal in all other aspects except for the OCD. Like we always say in the meetings, "It's [the OCD] like a monkey on the back that is always there."

I've really come so far though. I've made all of these friends and I no longer am gripped by the obsession with my eyes. I feel that it's totally lifted. I do realize though that this is a program of recovery and I will never be cured. I must continue to practice these steps to the best of my ability for the rest of my life or the disease can come back at me. I really do believe that.

There's a lot of talk about OCD being caused by a chemical imbalance in the brain. My personal theory about this is that it is possibly a chemical imbalance, but I believe that we trip the chemicals off with our emotions and our reactions. I believe that people with OCD hold on to resentments much more than the "average, normal person." People with OCD are more sensitive than other people, but by practicing the twelve steps, a person can come to like this more peaceful way of life. It's a character change in one's reactions to the things that happen. In other words, we no longer overreact to things because we're more centered. I think through the Program we keep this middle, average type road and we no longer get into those situations where we're mulling over things and we're holding onto resentments. We can keep our peace of mind.

I just know that the Program works and I love it. I do find that at times it's very hard though to stick with it because it really goes against today's society. It's a very "me, me, me" type of society and I believe we must also work with others to keep our "sobriety." We have to think of others every day and how we can be helpful to them. Sometimes, that's not easy to do. We want to be selfish and we want to go about and do our own thing, but we have to keep others in our minds. I'm grateful that I'm a part of OCA so that I have the opportunity to help others recover from OCD.

(3)
OCA Offered More Than OCD Relief

Obsessive Compulsive Disorder (OCD) has many different symptoms. I'm 21 and I have OCD. I experience the same pain as anyone else who has this disorder. Each person can have different symptoms, but we all experience the same kind of pain.

OCD not only hurts a person spiritually, mentally, and physically, but it also affects an individual's personality. Now I realize that I have many character defects. My OCD altered my perceptions and I became a selfish, uncaring walking time bomb. I was a very irritable person who could flare up in a second. In short, my personality was warped.

For as long as I can remember I've had OCD. It started out slowly and was not really dominating my life. I did little things like counting and checking. Eventually, though, things got worse. At first I thought my rituals were just bad habits. I tried to control my compulsions which only made them worse. Since I was a perfectionist I thought it was "normal" to check to make sure that everything in my closet was in order. At first I had spent only a few minutes checking, but eventually when things got really bad, I'd open and close the closet door about thirty times and then do the same with my bedroom door. I'd close it over and over again. I once opened and closed that door at least fifty times. When I finished that ritual, I knocked very hard on the door many times to make sure that it was closed. Then I would go downstairs only to have to go back up to make sure the door was closed. I used to cry a lot while I was peforming my rituals. When I entered Obsessive Compulsive Anonymous

(OCA) I felt hopeless.

I found out about the OCA program from a newspaper service column. Because the Program discusses the idea of a Higher Power, introduction into the group may be a bit difficult for some. This Higher Power doesn't necessarily have to be a conventional God or a religious figure. Your Higher Power can be the OCA group, or even nature. The main point is that it's a power outside of yourself. Many people may get turned off by that concept, but it's really important to stay as open-minded as possible and have the willingness to take actions toward recovery from OCD.

I didn't have a problem actually choosing a Higher Power of my understanding, but I still couldn't believe that an abstract power could relieve me of my obsessions if I couldn't do it myself. I was wrong!!

The Program also suggested that I read the literature, make phone calls and go to meetings. Basically, that I work and live in the 12 steps of recovery. However, initially I only worked some of these steps in my life. I didn't like the idea of making telephone calls, but sick people usually don't like healthy suggestions. I went to meetings and I sometimes read the books.

It took a while before I got any results at all from working the Program, and this made me feel worse. However, after two months I started feeling the effects of going to the meetings and OCD recovery. I finally had relief and felt so free and so good.

Not everyone is that fortunate. Don't be discouraged if your OCD symptoms don't subside immediately and you don't begin to see the results of recovery quickly. It takes longer for some people than for others. I know people who have taken two months to a year to "get the

Program." It's worth the wait though. I know I'm not finished with my recovery even though I've been in the Program for over a year. I try to work on my recovery every day.

When I have my "bad days" now, it's usually because I'm not working some aspect of my Program. As someone once told me, OCA is not a cure, but it sure offers, and gives, help and relief from OCD. If a person practices the principles of this simple, but not easy, program, that person can be sure to get results, even it it takes a while.

I know that I have gotten relief because now I do make the phone calls, read my books, listen, and often follow suggestions from other OCA members, as well as take my own inventory.

If you are wondering what it means to "take an inventory," to me it means getting rid of the time bomb inside of me as well as acknowledging, admitting and ultimately getting rid of my harmful resentments. The Big Book of Alcoholics Anonymous even states that resentments are the number one offender and a person must part with them if that person is to live a life of recovery. After one year I'm finally starting to let go of my resentments even though I never *really* wanted to get rid of them. Parting with my resentments towards other people has not only created a greater peace within myself, but has also enabled me to become a more caring person.

The program recommends that I listen to people and take suggestions. When someone suggested that I lead a meeting, I felt that I would actually faint if I spoke in front of a group. I took this person's suggestion and did it anyway. Now I'm very glad that I did. It's uncomfortable for me to lead a meeting because I have a hard time talking in front of crowds. However, if I want to recover, I must do what I don't always want to do, such as leading meetings and making telephone calls. I've also learned that these calls not only help me, but they help the other person too. It's amazing what the Program has done for me. This is a simple Program but it's definitely not an easy one. If I can help another OCD sufferer to feel better simply by making a phone call or saying something at a meeting, I feel great and at peace. Before, I just wanted things for myself and didn't care about anyone else. It's in helping others that I can stay in recovery. I must give it away in order to keep it . . . that feels good. I am so much better off than I was last year. I'm not saying that I'm perfect because I now know that I will never be perfect. I still have many things to work on. I get lazy and I have my "bad days" too, but if I didn't have the Program I might be in an insane asylum now. The Program works if you work it. All a person needs is an open mind, willingness and the desire to recover from OCD.

Even now I sometimes wait for results if a new obsession or compulsion appears. The best part though is that I have a terrific program that combats all aspects of my OCD. The Program is always there and it works. I can say this because I've experienced it. When I turn my OCD over to my Higher Power I get amazing results. When I work this Program, not only does my OCD become more manageable, but I live in a more positive way.

Even after I entered OCA I became afraid of contracting AIDS. However, I was relieved of this obsession after only three days of becoming involved in the Program. I don't think I will ever be cured of OCD, but I do believe that we can all live in recovery from this disorder and become better, happier and sane people.

I feel blessed to have OCD since it's because of this painful disorder that I have found the OCA Program and have become a better, less selfish and more caring person. So, the bottom line is that a person can live a life of recovery from OCD if that person gives himself to this simple Program.

(4)
It Took 12 Steps to Live with "13"

I was born on November 14, 1963. I have had OCD for about seven years and I have suffered tremendously.

I was approximately twenty years old when I began to develop a fear of the number thirteen. Whenever I saw the number thirteen, in any form, I felt totally contaminated. This included the time appearing on a clock, such as 3:13, as well as 1:00 P.M. which I converted in my mind into the thirteenth hour. I felt totally contaminated when the change I received was 13 cents or 13 dollars, as well as when it was the 13th day of the month or when I read words consisting of 13 letters. The pain brought on by this feeling of contamination consumed my entire being.

For the first five years I felt that I could conquer this fear on my own. I was never more wrong. I tried to convince myself that I could handle this . . . that it would go away . . . it didn't. Instead, it began to develop into some sort of monster that now controlled more and more of me. One day, while at the barber for a haircut, I had 13 dollars in my possession. At that time I thought nothing of this. Immediately after having my hair cut I felt that I was totally consumed with evil contamination. The only means that I felt I could use to rid myself of this evil feeling was to continue to get my hair cut. I was now going to the barber every 14 days or less. Not only did I begin to look ridiculous, but my barber could not understand why I felt that I needed to get my hair cut so often. A peach had more fuzz on it. I felt embarrassed, ashamed and completely lost. I knew I could no longer attempt to handle this problem on my own. Was I crazy? I wondered what was wrong with me. Do other people ever get like this? Who could I talk to? Who would believe me? I began to think that I must be crazy or perhaps I had a brain tumor. I knew that I had to seek help . . . but where would I start? I turned to my local telephone directory to see if anything was listed beginning with the word "phobia." Yes, there was a name for my condition. It's known as Obsessive Compulsive Disorder (OCD).

I was lucky. I found a therapist who referred me to a psychiatrist and I began treatments with both of these professionals.

Initially, I was seeing my therapist once a week and my psychiatrist every other week. At least four times a week I was attending a support group for people that suffer from OCD. They too offered me tremendous support. After 16 months of seeing my therapist, I was able to discontinue these visits. Presently, I see my psychiatrist once a month. I attend group a minimum of 2 times per week.

Sharing my feelings with other OCD sufferers has helped me realize that I am not alone. Approximately 4 million Americans suffer from some sort of Obsessive Compulsive Disorder. I was fortunate to realize, when I did, that I needed help. I'm eternally grateful to all the people who have worked, and continue to work, with me to help me conquer this illness. I am especially grateful to my parents for standing by me with their continued love and support. I am also extremely grateful to the people at my Thursday evening Obsessive Compulsive Anonymous (OCA) meeting. This group of people whom I love very much has helped me tremendously . . . they've saved my life.

Through the miracles of modern medicine, therapy,

and OCA, I am now able to feel relief from my obsession. My life has turned around completely, but that does not mean that at this time I am cured because I am not. I will always go to OCA meetings because there I have a fellowship that I can count on.

(5)
One 'Strand' At A Time

I can't think of any one time or single place that it all began. I only know that my rebirth happened last March, 1989. I can remember as a child performing the ritualistic behavior of bumping my head all night on my pillow. My mother used to come into my room during the middle of the night to wake me up to stop me from bumping my head which shook the bed frame and woke up my parents. Since I was asleep, I didn't even know that I was doing it. I felt that I just had to bump my head on the pillow. Consequently, I developed a crooked nose which was reshaped when I had a rhinoplasty at the age of 16.

I can remember twisting my hair from 7 years old until I was about 11 or 12 when I recall pulling it out by the roots and watching it fall on the floor strand by strand, pile by pile, not really wondering anything about it. I just knew that I had to do it and it felt good. It wasn't until I was around 14 or 15 years old that I started getting bald spots. My mother noticed them and began getting concerned. Since I told her that I would stop, I became very secretive and pulled my hair when no one was around.

I can't remember too much about the whens, the hows and the whats during my teenage years, but I do remember that I had the worst self-image in the entire world and I hated myself. When I was 15, I enrolled in a private school to improve my grades. I was a very ugly teenager and the boys in school always laughed at me.

It's hard to think of all of the different times and places of pain and humiliation, wearing wigs and trying to say, "I do this thing." I remember going to the hairdressers who often said, "I don't recall ever seeing anything like this before." Sometimes I wished I had cancer just so I'd have an excuse. Although there were a couple of understanding hairdressers who would work with me, there were others that were mean and would just insult me.

I guess the worst period was from about 15 to 25 years old. I just kept pulling and pulling and it got worse and worse. When I was in college, the spots on either side of my head above my ears were awful. I never wanted to pull the hair in the back of my head, but I always pulled on the sides, and sometimes on the top of the crown and in the front. I thought it was just a habit, like sucking your thumb, nail biting or smoking cigarettes, except I just couldn't stop. I suppose the worst part was that I couldn't find anyone else who also did this.

Consequently, I felt worthless because I believed that no man would want to date a woman with a bald head. I was very emotionally immature and sheltered throughout my whole life. I never wanted to do anything or go anywhere, nor did I excel in anything. My parents really didn't encourage me to do anything so I just sort of grew up feeling very mixed up inside. I remember that each time I reached out to somebody for help, love or understanding, the door would slam shut in my face. Naturally, that didn't help to alleviate my compulsion.

I had a couple of close friends but I wasn't popular and I certainly wasn't pretty. I'll never forget the day in sixth grade when my mother sent me out of the house with a plaid skirt and a striped blouse. When I got to school the kids laughed at me all day because my clothes were so uncoordinated.

I guess I was always jealous of my mother because she was so beautiful and I wasn't. I suppose you could say that trichotillomania [hair pulling] was partly self-mutilation because I knew that I would never be pretty so I felt that I might as well continue to pull my hair out. No matter how many theories there may be about this, all I know is that I couldn't stop pulling my hair out. My mother yelled and screamed at me and I cried because I couldn't stop pulling my hair. She sent me to a psychiatrist who told me what it was, but didn't offer any good suggestions, behavior therapy or other treatments to help me stop pulling my hair. I guess I can't really blame him though because at that time, twenty years ago, they didn't know anything about this stuff. Sometimes I think back and wonder if Howard Hughes would have lived a more fulfilling life had medical research been more advanced. Would any of us have lived a more fulfilling life? But I can't look back; I just have to take my experience and move on.

I want to reach out to other people, to the little girl who's pulling her hair out and say, "there's hope. You're not alone." One of our OCA groups in Pittsburgh is strictly for people with trichotillomania. Through this group, I've developed a network of other hair pullers and their families. It's been one of the most rewarding things I've ever done. I've made friends with a 16 year old member and another person who's 11, who are very severely stricken with this disease. I keep telling them not to give up because as research progresses there will hopefully be a solution to this problem. I've told them that I'm going to just keep praying for them until something happens in God's time because I know what they're going through. The change happened for me and I somehow believe that it's going to happen for them.

I think a lot about my OC family of checkers, washers, car drivers who are afraid that they've run somebody over, ruminators, contamination obsessors, perfectionists, people who want to be in control, people who constantly take their clothes on and off, people who are constantly picking their feet or their fingers and those people who are still in pain who I haven't met yet because they're too sick to come to group. I think about my OC family constantly. One might say that I obsess about OCD, but when a person doesn't know what he or she has, and after 35 years finally finds out that there are millions of people out there who have OCD and do the same things, it's like suddenly finding out that you have polio and then learning that Dr. Salk developed a vaccine for it.

When I think of all the research that's going on now, I realize that the children who've got OCD and the adults that suffer from symptoms don't have to suffer through years of agony with this disease any more. Nevertheless, the OCD life is a lonely life until one meets the OC family. I can honestly say that the past 12 months have been both the greatest and worst months of my life. They have been the greatest because of all the wonderful people that I've met and the work that I've been able to do to get the word out to other people with OCD. I marvel at all of the different sufferers who I've been able to find, those who have found us, and some of the recoveries that are starting to happen. There is nothing in the world more fantastic and helpful to a person's recovery than watching another sufferer recover.

I guess the painful part is when a person begins going through his or her own changes and starts to recover it's hard for other people, whether it be friends, co-workers, acquaintances, family, and especially one's spouse or significant other because the person that they fell in love with is no longer the same person.

When a person is part of a 12 step program, that person becomes completely new once the recovery process begins. The Program just totally turns a person's life around, and it's very hard to continue a relationship because that person is just not the same as before. In that respect, these past 12 months have been the worst because I know recovery work is what I want to do for the rest of my life. At 36 finding myself suddenly turning around and saying to my husband, "I know what I'm going to do" is very scary, especially when he doesn't suffer with OCD and doesn't understand what I'm going through.

I've been in remission since August 4th, 1989. My basic avenues of recovery have been my faith in my Higher Power, which for me is God, my OC family, my support groups and lastly, my medication.

Through my recovery I've learned not to try to be such a perfectionist but just to be me. I know that I will never give up my faith or my OC family; they've meant my rebirth. I especially appreciate the work and support that we've all gotten from the OC Foundation, Obsessive Compulsive Anonymous and the Pittsburgh Self-Help Group Network. The tireless members of these organizations have shown me the way to finding new energies and a new person in myself, who's always learning, growing and open to new ideas.

(6)
It Works

I have suffered from OCD since early childhood. I remember at an early age having to memorize TV commercials and going over them in my mind before going to sleep at night. I also had stuffed animals that I had to arrange in a particular order each day. In my way of thinking I did these things to keep something bad from happening to my parents. At about the age of fourteen I had a fear that my parents would turn into animals if I did not think positive thoughts about them. I have since learned that this is called magical thinking.

In the afternoons, after school, I went to my room, closed my door and went through thoughts and feelings that I felt needed to be straightened out in my mind. Perfectionism was involved with the OCD too. I was trying to actually make myself have good thoughts and feelings.

I married immediately after high school at an early age. My husband was a sick person also. He abused me throughout the marriage. This relationship lasted for eleven years until I finally left with our two beautiful children. My self-esteem was already low from the OCD, but now it was even lower from the abuse. I started using alcohol to help alleviate fears and worries.

I met my present husband about a year later. He had an alcohol problem too. We've been married for ten years and he has recently stopped drinking. My drinking is also under control. I used alcohol as a self-medication for the OCD. Although I got a little relief with the alcohol sometimes, at other times the liquor just made the OCD worse. As a person with OCD, the depression that alcohol caused was devastating to me since depression is usually associated with the disease also.

I started seeing a psychiatrist over a year ago who advised me to attend AA (Alcoholics Anonymous) meetings to help the OCD and the alcohol problem. I went to a lot of meetings, enjoyed the fellowship and learned a bit about the twelve-steps.

A friend who has OCD and I started an OCA group several months ago in our area. About seven people attend the meeting regularly. The fellowship is great and together we are learning to use the steps in our lives. As we grow, learn, and attend these meetings, they are becoming a great benefit to all of us in the group. Recently my OCD symptoms went into remission. I owe my thanks to the OCA program through which I was able to make the changes necessary to further my recovery.

(7)
Stop Worrying So Much

I know that I have never in my life really felt peace. I also know that at every moment there's been at least one thing that I worried about intensely or something that I got "stuck on." For months I worried and worried about this one thing. It was usually something that I felt guilty about doing when I was a small child. Perhaps I threw a piece of litter down the sewer, picked up a dirty clothespin off the bargain store floor and carried it home, or got a postcard for the discount price when the others were not on sale. These things produced years of worry with the fear that the police would come after me. The ultimate fear though, sitting in the back of my mind, was that I would someday end up being executed for murder. This fear was so frightening to me that I didn't want to go on vacations to states that had the death penalty just in case something happened. I knew at a very young age just which states these were.

I don't think I had a lot of rituals as a child. It was mostly the thoughts that drove me crazy. I do remember, though, holding my breath or spitting when I passed a cemetery. Also, every night when I was young, as early as I can remember, I went over a litany with my mom in which I had to ask her, "Is there nothing to worry about? Even a, b, c (whatever the specifics were at the time?)" She'd say, "Yes, there's nothing to worry about."

For as long as I can remember I have been afraid of being alone with my thoughts. Family vacations were awful because of the long period of time in the car when I couldn't read (being carsick or it was dark), nobody was talking and I was left alone for long periods of time with just my own thoughts. It was awful.

At home, when I went to sleep I used to listen to records from all the great musicals. Then I memorized all of them, even the really complicated ones like the opening to The Music Man with all of its parts...I still remember a lot of it. I also remember when we went to see the total eclipse on Cadillac Mountain and they talked so much about not looking directly at the sun during the eclipse that I then started worrying that maybe I had done it wrong. All night in the tent I kept getting terrified and asking them to turn on the lights. Each time I was relieved to find that I wasn't blind (yet). But a few minutes later it would seem to get darker and darker... my brother got pretty annoyed with me.

Anyway...does this mean that I have OCD??? Is that what was going on all along? Maybe so. I guess it probably was. I have always just thought that I was a person who worried a lot. From my earliest teacher conferences (around kindergarten or first grade) all my teachers told my mom that I was doing great but that I had to stop worrying so much. (Apparently, I had announced to my kindergarten or first grade classmates during show-and-tell that an atom bomb had been discovered and we were all going to die.)

When I sought professional help later, in high school and college, the school psychologist and the chaplain told me that I just needed to stop worrying so much. I was so smart and so functional. I was the head of every school and I went to a top university. How disturbed could I really be?? I never knew HOW to stop worrying. I think I started to wonder, if I was O.K., then why was I so unhappy?

I have always looked at each of my worries as individual problems, but to say that I have OCD seems to say that maybe what seems to be the problem isn't as much the problem as the way my mind works and interprets things. That's confusing to me.

To say that I have a disease of sorts is really comforting in a way, if I could be cured. But I don't know what that would look like and I can't really imagine it. I am so used to feeling badly about myself that it actually feels somewhat sinful to TRY to feel better.

The idea in Obsessive Compulsive Anonymous that nobody, or nothing in particular is to blame for this is also a radically different idea for me. I've spent twelve years in therapy trying to understand myself. I've gotten support through the pain and I've learned to be more assertive and more articulate about my feelings. I don't regret any of the time I spent with good therapists, but nobody ever made the pain go away. I have never been able to stand on my own and take the pain, or make decisions for myself without actually going nuts. This has been a source of great shame. I had really hoped for the "Freudian Miracle"; that I would one day figure out what horrible thing happened in my early childhood that made everything go awry. I have always held a dream of hypnosis or regression therapy as a last resort . . . to just grit my teeth and go back there and find out what the hell *it* was and get *it* over with, no matter how painful it is. But what if there never was an *IT?*

Today I had a good morning and enjoyed spending time with my baby. The time flew and I didn't sit around in a slump wondering how I was going to get through the day. I started thinking that maybe I don't really have OCD. I haven't been obsessive in a while (since yesterday). But then I went out with the baby and while I was parking someone squeezed by. I heard a noise and I couldn't stop wondering if our cars had scraped, and would I know it if they had? If they had, was it my responsibility? Should I do anything about it?...and so on and so on. After I took the baby for her checkup, I called my husband from a pay phone (across the street where no one could hear what I was saying because they might either think I was a dangerous driver or else I was nuts for asking him) and just double checked with him. If I had talked to myself a lot, or had been in a better mood, I probably could have lasted without asking him and getting his reassurance. If not, perhaps I could have at least waited until he got home. It did give me peace right then and there to get it off my mind. I guess I must have OCD...

I was asked to share my "experience, strength and hope" with readers of this book. I feel like I am a real beginner here. I don't know how my story will turn out, but I do have a great deal of hope, and I *CAN* talk about *that.* For the first time in my life I have found people who seem to understand the particular pain I have always carried with me. They know what I mean when I tell my story. While our particular obsessions may differ greatly, the pain, frustrations, fears and shame involved in having OCD seem to be strikingly similar for all of us. For the first time, I can admit to myself and to others the "crazy" thoughts and actions that take hold of my life. I can begin to feel what it is like not to feel shame. I can even enjoy being laughed at, lovingly, by people in the group who can point out the ridiculousness of my fears while they understand the depth of my pain and the grip that these fears have on my life. Between my psychiatrist, my therapist, the OCA group and ACOA (Adult Children of Alcoholics) group that I attend, I actually feel, for the first time, that I have a real support network. Each one of them supports my work with the others because they all have a similar philosophy. Each support system encourages me to do everything I can to work on my recovery by using behaviour therapy, medication, the twelve steps and the support of the community. For the first time, I am beginning to hope there is something I can do to become freer, with the help of others, instead of just waiting for one obsession to replace another so I can have that temporary period of relief when I get rid of the old one. For the first time, I am beginning to hope for some sort of real healing. I am encouraged to transform my way of living and thinking, rather than weathering out each period of clinical depression and hoping that the next one will not come soon. For the first time, I am beginning to feel that I am not alone, and maybe I never need to be alone again.

(8)
From Fear to Faith

"You are not an alcoholic," the clinical psychologist stated firmly. "Yes, I am," I retorted. "Your problem is not alcohol." "Please don't tell me I'm not an alcoholic," I begged, then added, "It's taken me too long to get sober as it is." "You can believe you're an alcoholic if you want to, but I'm telling you alcohol is not your main problem."

That was December, 1976. I had been sober through the program of Alcoholics Anonymous for a year by then. I was living in a half-way house for alcoholic women and going to A.A. meetings daily. I was quite sore by the time I left the psychologist's office that afternoon. In fact, I had made up my mind that if she couldn't believe I was an alcoholic, I would not go back to see her.

My vocational rehabilitation counselor had difficulty understanding why I was so upset with the psychologist, and insisted I see her again. He assured me the doctor was sorry she'd upset me and would apologize to me; but I had to go back to see her again. She was treating me for my severe handwashing compulsion and my fears of contamination. The odd thing about my visit with her that day was that she did not tell me what my main problem was — that I have Obsessive Compulsive Disorder.

I know today that the doctor was right — but only partially right. I am an alcoholic. I was unable to stop drinking when I wanted to. It took me almost two years in A.A. to be able to stop completely. But OCD is my main problem.

Looking back over my life, I have to admit that I have always been insecure and afraid. My earliest memory is one of fear. I was anxious and unable to relax, even as a child.

I was born in Pittsburgh, Pennsylvania, the third of seven girls. The family moved to Florida when I was five years old. My father is an alcoholic who got very violent when he drank, and my mother has had nervous problems. As a child, I remember hearing stories about my mother being on the verge of a nervous breakdown when I was born. I heard gruesome accounts of the horrible pain I put my mother through, and how I resisted the doctors' best efforts to bring me into the world. I ended up feeling guilty just for being alive. Still I didn't blame my mother. Growing up, I thought she was a saint. She seemed so perfect. I wanted to be just like her. I was afraid of my father, as he made what I considered unreasonable demands on me and my sisters, expecting us to act like adults instead of children. We were often berated and whipped with belts. My parents fought constantly and I stayed upset over it. I was brought up Catholic and was a very religious child. I was well-liked by both my classmates and teachers at parochial school, despite my timidity.

My OCD surfaced around the age of eight. I was very obsessed with doing the right thing — always. I had a terrible fear of sinning, and constantly worried about displeasing God and going to hell. It seemed as though the harder I tried to be good, the worse I felt about myself. As the years went by, it seemed things just got worse. I found myself plagued with constant doubt. Going to confession on Saturday afternoon was a particular problem because no matter how thorough I had been, I never felt right (nor forgiven, for that matter) once I stepped out of the confessional. I was terrified that once I stepped outside the front door of the church I was going to drop dead on the steps. At first, I could resist going back into the church after confession, but as time went on I found myself going back and forth through the doorway without knowing why.

It was around this time that my hair pulling began. It started one day while I was sitting at my desk in school. I pulled out my hair at the crown, and then bit the roots off of each piece. Once I started, I was unable to stop when I wanted to. I ended up with bald spots on the top of my head, which I had to cover up. Later, I pulled out my eyebrows. I was so ashamed of myself, and could not understand why I couldn't stop pulling my hair.

At age twelve I decided I wanted to be a nun. My sixth grade teacher was such a wonderful one. I remember thinking that being a nun was probably the closest thing you could get to being a saint. I began saving my pennies in a coffee can so I could join the convent, because I knew my parents couldn't afford to send me.

Somewhere around this time, my parents divorced. At first, I really expected to feel better, as I no longer had to be around my father, and the threat of constant violence was gone. Instead, I began to fear that I was going insane. One night, out of desperation, I went to my mother and asked her to send me to see a psychiatrist. She said I didn't need one. There was little relief in her words. I was hurt and confused; I was sure she couldn't be blind to all my troubles. Didn't she know I was different? Couldn't she see the agony I was going through? Perhaps I'd been better at acting than I thought, as I had often tried to keep my problem a secret.

I began to drink when I turned seventeen years old. Up until then I'd been reluctant to drink (even at family dinners, etc.) because of the way alcoholism had destroyed my parents' marriage. But by seventeen my myriad fears and doubts were my constant companions. I couldn't shake them, and I stayed depressed much of the time. Drinking was fun at first, though I drank like an alcoholic from the start. It didn't take long for me to become really sick from alcohol; two months short of turning twenty-one, I attended my first A.A. meeting. Things did not go well for me in the beginning, and I drank again. I could see that the program worked for others, but I was not sure it could work for me.

During my early days in the program, I got professional help for the first time. I had counseling on and off, was put on medication, lived in a halfway house three different times, and attended meetings. Nothing seemed to help much. I ended up in the detox unit several times, the hospital twice for severe depression, and I overdosed once on a mixture of pills and booze. I also noticed I was spending an abnormal amount of time washing my hands and worrying about contamination.

I had my last drink on December 5, 1975. To this day, I believe that God was really looking out for me that night. I had set out to drink myself to death, for I thought I was fighting a losing battle. When I awoke the next morning, there were beer cans and half-burned cigarettes in the bed. I knew then that I had reached a turning point. I could not go on the way I was living. I needed help, and fast. I called A.A. again, and two dear ladies came out and talked to me, convincing me to go back into the halfway house and to get involved in A.A. I'm glad I listened to them, and am happy to say that I am now sober for a little over fourteen years.

I have only known about my Obsessive Compulsive

Disorder for about a year now. I do not know why I was never told that I have OCD. Perhaps the psychiatrists just didn't know it. I found out what my problem was from watching the Phil Donahue show on OCD.

Throughout the process of recovery, my greatest fear was that I was going crazy. While Alcoholics Anonymous helped me to get my life together once I stopped drinking, it could not cure my OCD. After being sober about a year, my handwashing compulsion improved, but my OCD just expressed itself in other ways. I found myself constantly worrying about something bad happening, and then the checking began. I have been a checker for a very long time. There were times when my checking got so bad that I would be screaming inside, and at the same time I would beg God to take me or change me; I could not go on this way. In April, 1989, I made an appointment to see the doctor. I ended up telling him about my OCD. He seemed to have trouble understanding just how bad off I was. My husband had just been told he had a tumor and that it was most likely cancer. He was going to have to have surgery, and soon! I was a total wreck and was seeing danger in everything. The doctor gave me a prescription and I took it. At first it seemed to help, like the other medications I have had, only to make me feel worse the longer I took it. I stopped taking it.

I have always believed in God. My trouble since getting sober has been in trusting God to work things out for me. This has not stopped me from praying, and I cried with joy when we learned that my husband's tumor was benign.

My A.A. sponsor told me about the Recovery, Inc., Program, and encouraged me to attend. I went and felt the program was good. I did feel better when I went.

Unaware of Obsessive Compulsive Anonymous' existence, I had wished there was a place for people like me to go for direct help with my specific illness. Around this time, a letter appeared in the Ann Landers column in our local newspaper giving the address for the Obsessive Compulsive Foundation, as well as information on the work being done there. My husband brought the letter to my attention, encouraging me to write the Foundation. He insisted that they might be able to help me.

I put off writing for about a week. I'm not sure why, except perhaps I had some doubts that even they could help me. After all, everything else I had tried had failed. I still pulled my hair, breaking each strand into ten pieces, still feared contamination (though the handwashing was under control for the most part), still had terrible fears of death and/or of something horrible happening if I didn't recheck things, or if I drove an automobile.

My husband stood by me through it, though I'm sure it was hell for him at times. I never realized until recently how difficult it is for those who love us to live with us. It can't help but affect them, too.

The OC Foundation got me in touch with two wonderful women in the area also suffering from OCD. Up until then, I had never known but one other person with the disorder. Over the next few weeks, I kept in touch with these two OCD sufferers via the telephone. We all agreed we needed help, that it was a great feeling to know we weren't alone anymore, and that we needed the support of each other. Throughout this time, I talked on about how wonderful it would be if there was an organization like A.A. for OCD sufferers. None of us were aware then that OCA existed. The answer to my prayers came when a friend of mine in whom I had confided about my OCD brought me an article from First Magazine. There was a New York address for OCA in it. I was so excited that I wrote a letter to New York at once. Our kind friends in New York replied at once, and granted us permission to start a group in Florida. Since I had helped start A.A. groups in Florida, I knew what needed to be done. I set about looking for a room we could meet in, and within two weeks, we had a place plenty large enough for the four of us to meet. I already had an A.A. Big Book, and the Twelve and Twelve, and my sponsor and friend volunteered to bring the coffee pot. On November 7, 1989, we met for the first time, in a church in Rockledge, Florida. Thus, the Hope Group of Obsessive Compulsive Anonymous came into existence.

Today, I am truly grateful that OCA exists, and for the first time I have hope for a brighter future and a happy life. It is such a relief to know what is wrong with me, and that I can get better. I know how well the twelve steps work for alcoholism and I have faith that they will work just as well for my OCD. Although I am still very new to OCA, I have had a reduction in some of my symptoms, and my hair pulling compulsion has been lifted. I can relax, knowing everything is okay.

I am going to stay active in both my programs, as I believe that working with others will help me to get well. I know today that worry and trust do not go together. I have turned my life and will over to my Higher Power, and know that it is with Him that they rightly belong. After all, He didn't bring me this far to let go of me now.

(9)

My Secret

Outwardly, I appear to be a normal suburban house-wife, your typical nice Italian Catholic girl married to a nice Jewish dentist. We have two healthy, terrific sons, a six-year-old and a four-year-old. But inside, I carry a secret I've kept for over twenty-five years; I live the tortured life of a sufferer of OCD. Peace of mind, something most people take for granted, has not totally been mine since I was an adolescent (when this problem emerged).

My OCD has taken many forms, including obsessive thoughts, scrupulosity, excessive handwashing, excessive housecleaning and excessive checking. This has made my life so unbearable that at times I've thought it would be better to be dead; then I might find the peace I so desperately want.

Like so many sufferers of OCD, I'm embarrassed and ashamed of the things I find it necessary to do. I've hidden as much of this behavior as I possibly could from friends, neighbors, co-workers and the people I love most. Like so many others with this affliction, I have been amazingly good at this deception. I've kept my OCD a secret from my sister-in-law, who is one of my closest confidantes and a psychiatric nurse, for approximately twenty-three years. I would tell someone I had to get something in my car, when my real purpose was to go check for the millionth time to see if the doors were locked. I would excuse myself to go to the bathroom, when my real purpose was to be alone so I could figure out whether an obsessive thought I had had was a mortal sin according to the teachings of the Roman Catholic Church.

Innately knowing this behavior is ludicrous hasn't stopped me. I'm compelled to do what I do. It hasn't even mattered that a compulsion is exhausting; I've still continued to do it. One night at the end of the school year, I stayed up practically all night, checking and rechecking my class attendance register to be sure it was correct. There were 180 boxes for each of my homeroom students, one box for each day of the school year. I had over twenty-five students. I had worked all day, then did this exhausting task and got to bed at approximately five-thirty in the morning. I got perhaps one and a half hours of sleep, got up and went to work the next day. To this day I don't think my husband has any idea I got so little sleep that night. I was six months pregnant with my first child at the time.

The hours I've spent agonizing over supposed sins I've committed are horribly painful for me to think about. I'll never forget the time I went to confession twice before I received communion on Easter Sunday. I've checked, rechecked then checked that I've rechecked store receipts. I've done this, not to be sure I wasn't overcharged or shortchanged, but rather, to be as positive as I possibly could be that I wasn't undercharged or given too much change.

OCD has prevented me from leading a full, productive and good life. I'm now in a Twelve-Step Program with others who share this vicious illness. Because of the people I've met in Obsessive Compulsive Anonymous, I'm not alone in my secret, painful world anymore. I've actually met and talked to people who the unbelievable has happened to: people who are in recovery from OCD.

The best possible life that I can dream of, hope for, and pray for is a life in recovery from OCD. I don't want more money, a bigger and better house, an expensive car; I just want freedom from this jail in my psyche. I want to be able to take my children to the playground, library, and soccer practice without constant worry. I want to be able to read them their bedtime stories without frightening obsessive thoughts racing through my mind. With recovery, I could be a better wife and mom to the most important people in my life. I know God wants me to work at this Twelve-Step program, and to get whatever help I need, medical or otherwise, in order to be healthier.

I can say at this early stage that our program is starting to help me achieve some measure of serenity — something I've so desperately wanted in my life. I find myself with a greater acceptance of people and circumstances over which I have no control. Feeling of frustration and anxieties are being replaced with a greater peace of mind. I think this is because I trust in my Higher Power, God, and his will for me. I'll always be a member of OCA — it's there that I belong.

(10)
A Painful Struggle

I have had OCD for as long as I can remember. My teen years were very difficult because that's when my OCD really became obvious to me. I began checking and rechecking certain things. I also started a pattern of repeating things four times.

Growing up I knew that there was something wrong, but I was always able to live with the strange things that I did. Up until last year, as time went on, nothing changed. My two main problems continue to be my repeating and my constant checking. I have some days that are fine but there are other days when my OCD rituals feel unbearable. My feelings about myself are very low and I feel that I do everything wrong.

I am constantly checking such things as the car door to assure that the light is off when I close the door, or my alarm clock to guarantee that it is set correctly for the next day. I could go on and on describing my ritualistic behaviors. Once I start checking I can't do anything to control myself; I become obsessed with these rituals.

I have learned that I cannot fight OCD alone. Once I get started, there is no turning back. I feel that I must complete my ritual.

I also feel compelled to repeat things. I am constantly repeating things to my wife, but manage to say the same thing again using different words if she becomes annoyed.

Through the years I have been to two psychiatrists. Although at the time I was sure that I was having a heart attack, I was also hospitalized for what turned out to be an anxiety attack.

One year ago I joined a 12-step program for OCD,

which I've been attending once a week ever since Although I still have my compulsions, and I don't believe that I'll ever be totally cured of OCD, I feel that the meetings have helped reduce the rituals.

It's wonderful to be able to talk to people with similar problems without feeling embarrassed. I have met some very nice people in the rooms who suffer the same pain as I do. The meeting gives us an opportunity to get together and share with each other what we are going through.

I have recently started taking anti-obsessional medication to combat some of the OCD symptoms. Although I have avoided using medications throughout the years, I now feel that the combination of the 12 step program and this medication offers me a greater opportunity to enjoy things more and live a happier life.

(11)
A Simple Letter?

What a wonderful time my girlfriend and I had last night! I love her very much. The next day I found a love letter in the mailbox from her. It was a nice surprise — until I had what I call a "thought attack." My mind began to race with fear: "I must contact her to express my gratitude for the letter"... "What if I say something wrong?"... "My voice may crack or the inflection of my words may be inappropriate"... "I just know I'm going to ruin this beautiful relationship I've found"...

Finally, through careful (and I mean careful in the most agonizing sense of the word) thought, I come up with an idea. I'll send her a letter and postscript it with "I'll call you tomorrow, Sweetie." This will buy me some time. I write the letter. The process is emotionally exhausting. I have to read the letter over and over again, until I am sure I have not written anything inappropriate, hurtful, or destructive to the relationship. Although I have read it no less than fifteen times, I still have many doubts about what I have written. I still don't know whether I have written something that will ruin my new relationship. My doubting is my disease. I feel like crying.

Finally, I leave for my girlfriend's house. I have to make sure she is not home. After calling and getting no answer, I drive over. I am afraid I will drive by her on the road and then my great plan will collapse. I'm afraid if I run into her, I will say something inappropriate and lose her. The drive over is agonizing. I'm filled with anxiety. I pull onto her street, terrified that I will meet her there, but I don't. I run out of my car and place the letter sticking out of the mailbox. It takes a minute just to make sure it is positioned correctly.

I leave, and get about three quarters of a mile away, when I become terrified that the postscript on the back of the envelope is not, "I'll call you tomorrow, sweetie," but something sick, inappropriate, perverse, or just plain crazy. I just don't know. I doubt and doubt. I drive back, read it over and over till I am convinced that all is well, and then go home. No sooner do I get home then I begin to doubt all that is written in the letter. Have I blown it? Did I write something inappropriate? My sleep is restless and terror-filled. I feel like my mind is torturing me. Please God, help me.

The next day I call her and discover she is sick. She doesn't fawn over me, and I become terrified that I have written something sick and distorted. I am exhausted.

That night I see her and, once again, she declares her love for me. The whole maze of worry I went through was groundless. Why does this go on? I am tortured by my own mind.

Meanwhile, all the time this has been going on I have also been counting and checking, compulsively closing the car door TWICE (it must be twice!). I check the car lights over and over again, touching the steering wheel twice, looking at the traffic light or a passerby twice. The counting and checking goes on as a background to my daily life, and even to the incident I have just described about my girlfriend. The process is a true nightmare, and I feel quite powerless to stop it all. If I try to stop my behavior, I get tremendous rushes of anxiety and fear.

Now I am in OCA and am also receiving medical attention. I have great hope that I will recover from this Obsessive Compulsive Disorder, and live in peace and joy with the woman I love. I know that without recovery I don't stand a chance. I am very relieved to have found Obsessive Compulsive Anonymous. I have great hope now!

(12)
My Own Private Hell

I don't know what the day or the date was, or the actual situation that had occurred. I do know that I had the feeling that something was not right; that *I* wasn't "quite right," — this feeling would stay with me for over ten years. I was a "picker." This might sound dumb, but it's true. I picked on myself by picking at my skin. Although most commonly at my face, I picked at whatever I thought didn't belong on any parts of my body. You see, I wanted to be perfect. I simply would not stand for having blemishes or flaws on myself, so the only thing for me to do was to get rid of them. This made perfect sense to me at the time, but after a while I realized that I couldn't stop. My favorite room in the house became the bathroom. I spent hours in there — just me, myself, and the soooo-dreaded mirror.

I examined myself intensely, not because I liked to but because I had to. Naturally, by the time I was finished, that part of my body that I picked (usually my face) was totally red. I fooled everyone ... except myself. When my mom asked, "What happened to your face?" I said that I was using a new face scrub or that I had used too much hot water, etc., etc.

I had all of the answers, except for why I was doing this outrageous crime to myself. I hadn't yet known about OCD. I only knew that when the picking started to get worse (such as my using pins and needles to dig at my skin) I needed help.

Once diagnosed as having OCD, my therapist exposed me to Obsessive Compulsive Anonymous (OCA). It was there that I met a group of people who shared a common disorder — the recurrence of obsessions and compulsions — and a common goal — to work together to make life more bearable.

It was recommended to me to buy the Alcoholics Anonymous (AA) book, *The Twelve Steps and Twelve Traditions.* I was told to substitute the word "alcohol" with the term "OCD," and to apply the steps to my own particular problem. I've gotten through half of the twelve steps but I need to go back and rework them.

Although I'm new in OCA, the Program has started to help me. Perhaps more helpful to me than the book has been the people in the OCA group. They are the ones who come each week to share their stories and offer bits of helpful suggestions. I am grateful to each one of these individuals.

Perhaps one day I'll start a group or try to reach out to someone else who is struggling with OCD. But, in the meantime, I'll stick to learning the twelve steps and attending weekly OCA meetings. At the very least, I know that I'm not alone. My own private hell isn't just mine. For once, it felt good to open up and tell other people that I've got this problem — this insane urge to hurt myself. It helps to know that there are people who understand and have gone the same route as I have.

Maybe someone who is reading this will identify with it. I hope not, for no one should go through the pain, but if you do, it's important to recognize that this problem is not unique. There are others who are suffering with it and who know about the pain and the guilt that you have. Above all, it's not your fault. For me that was reassuring.

It's up to me, and you, though, to do something

about it. Since it's true that there's "strength in numbers," we can work together to help each other battle this disease. The worst thing is thinking that you're the only one suffering with these compulsions and/or obsessions. Thank God, though, we know that this is not true. We are not alone.

(13)
Haunted By Fears

Writing this story is one of the most difficult, and yet one of the most beneficial things I've been asked to do. The difficulty, as well as the benefits arise from the necessity to truly confront the reality of my Obsessive Compulsive Disorder (OCD) and how it has affected my entire life. Within this past year (1989) I've actually become painfully aware that I have OCD. I can safely say that I have spent at least the last twenty-four years cowering to the whims of my OCD. I never stopped to consider that my behavior might have been somewhat bizarre, although I knew, even as a young child, that I was motivated to perform obsessive rituals solely on the basis of my fear . . . but fear of what, of whom? I had a vague sense that "something" mystical and animated, or "someone" cruel and hostile would "get me;" I performed strange behaviors to ward off the tragic outcomes I feared. I checked closets, underneath beds, outside second-floor windows, and anywhere else I may have contrived that these creatures or bogie-men could be hiding.

Although there was a great deal of unexpressed love and (somewhat overbearing) concern in my family, my home was noticeably filled with tension and fear. As the third and youngest of three daughters, I became abnormally dependent on my mother and emulated most of her fears while I silently created a plethora of my own.

I realize now that "magical thinking" has been associated with almost every action I've taken throughout my life. It would be fruitless to even begin to describe the barrage of obsessions and complementary rituals I have experienced. Suffice it to say that there have been plenty, ranging from the terror and panic ignited by not knowing how an object got lost or moved, to the need to say special prayers, or to say specific words a precise number of times.

As an easily impressionable teenager with a compulsive personality, I spent much of my high school and college days excessively drinking alcohol and abusing drugs. What I called "partying" was actually a means of covering up my feelings and avoiding reality. In many ways I believe my OCD has served, and often continues to serve, the same purpose. As I reflect back, I can see that it was quite a "trip" being incredibly high on drugs and drunk on whiskey while obsessing about how an object was moved, and performing rituals to avoid contact with that object. I also began bingeing and vomiting in college, and remained bulimic for the next five years. I now see that almost every time I began a cycle of bingeing and purging, I had eaten foods which my distorted thinking deemed as "jinxed" or "spooky" and therefore too harmful to remain in my body. It floors me to think of how insidious and destructive OCD can actually be.

As I let go of my bulimic behavior and my drug and alcohol abuse (from fear of eventually killing myself), I latched on to anorexia, with which I have been struggling ever since. Although it has taken on several different forms throughout the years, OCD has accompanied all of my various addictions and self-destructive actions.

I know today that I can't change what I have done, but I can affect what actions I take now. In 1982, when I stopped drinking alcohol and abusing drugs, I was fortunate enough to frequent many open Alcoholics Anonymous (AA) meetings and bear witness to the miracles of recovery. Since my eating disorder was my primary problem, I eventually became a member of

Overeaters Anonymous (OA).

The Twelve-Step Program has given me an opportunity to grow, emotionally and spiritually. As I apply the Program's principles to all areas of my life, I can actually see the process of recovery taking place. Although I'd been in OA (as well as psychotherapy) for over seven years it wasn't until this past year that I learned I have a disease believed to be caused by a biochemical imbalance. Until recently, I believed that my thoughts and behaviors were so bizarre that no one would understand them (especially since I didn't truly understand the nature of these obsessions and rituals myself). I tried to hide them and appear as normal as I possibly could. Needless to say, eventually family and friends did notice my strange actions, but either joked about them or denied that I could actually be behaving in such a strange manner. It wasn't until I accidentally slipped to my therapist about my "insane thoughts" that I learned that other people also suffer with obsessions and compulsions that they too feel powerless over.

After several months of strong denial, I finally surrendered to the reality that I had a disease which required as much, if not more, treatment than my eating disorder and other addictive behaviors. Following months of paralyzing anxiety attacks, I sought help from a behavior therapist who specializes in treating people with OCD. I began the flooding process which required me to directly and honestly confront my fears and refrain from performing rituals to counteract "potential doom."

The agony of OCD was so great that I thought I was willing to go to any lengths to lessen the pain and live my life more sanely. I mistakenly thought I had surrendered to the process of recovery, but soon learned that my fear-based willfulness to remain governed by the OCD was stronger than I had ever imagined. Eventually, however, because my life was so unmanageable, I began to risk challenging my unfounded fears and beliefs. Tackling OCD has been the hardest endeavor I've ever attempted. However, as I continue the process of facing my fears, I find my life becoming a bit more sane and my abilities revitalizing. Additionally, although I was initally quite opposed to taking medication, I have recently begun incorporating it into my recovery program.

By questioning and confronting my obsessive fears and their corresponding rituals, I have accomplished feats that I never thought possible. I know, though, that I could never have accomplished any of these things had I not trusted in the tools of the Twelve-Step Program to guide me.

As I began allowing myself to be humble about having the disease, I started selectively confiding in a few close program friends. Although I rationally understood that OCD is a biochemical disorder over which I am completely powerless by myself, emotionally I believed that I was quite deranged for having such strange thoughts and performing such bizarre rituals. Therefore, it was quite a risk for me to divulge my darkest secret, even to these friends, who knew more about me than many of my own family members.

Humbled by the pain of obsessing and ritualizing, I let go of the fear of judgment and rejection and gathered a haven of supportive people to help me along the path of recovery. Sharing my trepidation and terror with under-standing program friends before and after I abstained from performing a ritual took some of the power away from the disease; I felt more comforted, and even proud of myself. I also use the tool of writing to release my negative feelings and paralyzing fears. This helps me to quiet the chatter in my mind and alleviate the anxiety created by my OCD.

The support I received from knowledgeable and caring professionals, as well as family and friends, has encouraged me to continue my trek. I have found that speaking with others who have OCD has helped me tremendously and has enabled me to be more honest about my disease.

As I tackle some difficult OCD-related fears, the life-issues which these fears have masked for so many years are now surfacing, requiring me to acknowledge and deal with them. Although often terrifying, this has been an exciting and exhilarating process. I've also noticed that the path of recovery is not straight and smooth, but sometimes extremely bumpy.

As I have begun acting in a healthier manner I've noticed that the OCD is holding on, desperately trying to maintain its place in my life. I find this frustrating, but I am also grateful to have insight and awareness about it which I never had before.

I experience anger toward my obsessions and rituals because I truly want to live my life more fully without being robbed by this disease. Although I do not believe that I will ever be totally rid of the obsessions, I know that through perseverance, honesty and a willingness to work the Twelve-Step Program, my life can be fuller and more rewarding. I am extremely grateful to all those people who continue to stand by me and help me on my journey of recovery.

(14)
A Living Hell

The title of this story may sound dramatic to most readers, but it probably seems quite accurate to a person who has OCD.

I guess you would say that I'm a "checker" since that seems the most fitting label for my symptoms. I remember spending a lot of time as a child moving objects in my room and counting each time I moved something. There was no way I could leave my house for school unless I closed my dresser drawer a certain way and counted while doing that. Of course, this ritual varied from object to object and number to number.

As I got older, the checking of objects seemed to change to the checking of my own thoughts. Sometimes I thought about things people had said or experiences that I had and counted how many times I thought about them. While I was counting, a tremendous feeling of guilt and depression overcame me. I didn't know why this was happening but it just seemed impossible not to obsess.

When I became fourteen years old I started coming out of it. I made some new friends and things seemed to be looking up for me. My friends and I experimented with drugs and I found out quickly that drugs and OCD don't mix very well. The drugs made me feel important — like one of the guys.

I was always ready to go out with this group and try something new. One night we were experimenting. I wanted to show how "macho" I was so I took a double dose of what everyone else was taking. The next twelve hours were pure hell. When the drug wore off, I thought I had learned my vicious lesson, but the trouble was just beginning for me.

I began obsessing about this experience twenty-four hours a day, seven days a week. I was no longer able to go to the places that reminded me of that bad experience. However, the problem was that these places included my own house, my friends' houses, and practically everything in my neighborhood. I began eliminating each place and activity one by one because I feared each one so greatly. When I was around these stimuli I began to sweat, my heart raced, my ears rang, and my vision blurred. In the midst of what I later learned is called a panic attack, I lived and relived every day (sometimes four times daily) the feeling that I was going to die. This went on for the next fourteen years.

I consulted ear and eye doctors, practiced meditation, and read various self-help books. I learned a lot from a psychologist who I was seeing for four years but I was still obsessive and compulsive. Like most people stricken with a relentless depression, I considered suicide but that was too scary.

By that point I realized that I had virtually tried everything to relieve my torture. One day, as I was looking through a magazine for something to help me, I found an article about Obsessive Compulsive Anonymous (OCA). After attending my first meeting a tremendous weight was lifted from my shoulders. There were people at that meeting who understood what I was saying. For the first time in fourteen years I heard other people speaking about the same struggles I had experienced.

It was very difficult to speak in front of a group of people about something that had been a dark secret filled with fear and anxiety for so long. Looking out at the group though, I saw friendly, understanding faces. At that point I knew I had a chance.

By combining medication with my OCA meetings, I've experienced a good percentage of recovery and I've rediscovered serenity. With the help of my OCA friends I'm living a much fuller life now. I used to think that I wouldn't have a family, but I've been blessed with a beautiful, supportive wife and a son.

Every once in a while I think about my father who passed away engulfed in the horrors of OCD. He never had a chance since he never really knew what he had. I also think about the other people who are suffering with OCD unaware, and I pray that God will give them some direction.

To Our Families and Friends

Living with or being close to someone with OCD can be every bit as difficult as having the problem itself. However, it doesn't necessarily have to be. The same recovery program we have described here can also be used for the families and friends of those with OCD.

People closest to us have often tried every possible way to "break us" of our obsessions and compulsions. Some have gone to the extreme of doing our rituals for us or trying to make our environment "OCD free." Sadly this approach is *not* the solution. Family and friends must accept the fact they also are powerless over our obsessions and compulsions and they cannot help us by "taking on" our OCD. In program the term "enable" comes to mind here. By playing our OCD game with us, the family unknowingly "enables" us to continue our self-destructive behavior. Instead, "detaching" from their loved one's OCD can allow the family to heal even if the obsessive-compulsive behavior remains unchanged. This is not to say that the family doesn't love or feel for the sufferer; in fact the opposite is usually true. Family members must not try to shield us from the consequences of our OCD. No making excuses to the boss when we're late, no taking over our responsibilities that will clearly burden the family. Instead the family must work its program in spite of this illness. It is possible to love the individual while detaching from his sickness. The family doesn't have to suffer from the OCD.

Families seem to have also found it helpful to work the Twelve Step program in their lives. Instead of centering their lives around the OCD, families can work their program. Watching for resentment and fear can help heal a family torn by OCD. Belief in a Higher Power can restore a family to sanity and give new hope. Knowing that God runs the show can take the burden of responsibility off weary shoulders since no one is to "blame" for the OCD. Reaching out to other families whose lives have been changed by OCD can be the foundation of your recovery.

Now about the child whose parents have OCD. Although these children may not develop OCD they often will bear other scars. Rigid rules and unrealistic expectations become the norm in childhood. The parent's striving for control limits the child's freedom of choice. Often feelings of being trapped in the parent's cycle of illness will develop. Doing things outside the family's "boundaries" results in guilt so little is done to change the status quo. *As adults in recovery these people can learn to nurture their own needs as opposed to nurturing their parents' need for control.* This recovery for adult children of obsessive-compulsives also lies in the Twelve Step program and detachment from the OCD.

Now to the family whose member has found Obsessive Compulsive Anonymous: Be patient! This approach works for us on an individual time schedule. If your loved one has found OCA and intends to give it his best shot, recovery is likely. Let him spend as much time as he responsibly can with the program. Try not to feel jealous of his attention to OCA; this is how the fellowship works. Enthusiasm will help the obsessive-compulsive to recover since he will be willing to work the program harder.

We hope we have given you some good suggestions. Remembering that no one is responsible for another's recovery is essential. We are only responsible for our own recovery program.

Some Helpful Suggestions

1. - We utilize the program - not analyze it. The reasons why it works for us are not important - *what is important is that it works.*

2. - This is a "we" program - by attending meetings and getting active in OCA we recover together.

3. - At our meetings we emphasize our application of the 12 Step program to reduce our OCD. OCA is *not* a place to endlessly discuss our obsessions and compulsions. We *are* gathered to share our common *solution* to this problem - the 12 Step program.

4. - *Recovery* through OCA is defined as the relief obtained from our obsessions and compulsions as a result of working the 12 Step program. "Total abstinence" from OCD is *not* our focus - instead we focus on our daily application of program and its incorporation into our lives. This emphasis will result in a reduction of OCD symptoms and a state of well-being.

5. - OCA is not a psychological counseling service or do we make medical referrals. For information in those areas call the OC Foundation at (203) 772-0565 or write PO Box 9573, New Haven, CT 06535.

6. - Outside treatments for OCD are just that - outside treatments. We do not endorse or oppose specific outside treatments for OCD. We have found that those of us who are receiving medical or psychological treatments for OCD can work this program with good results. We ask our members *not* to discuss these treatments during our meetings. At OCA our focus is on the 12 Step program and how

we use it to gain relief from our OCD.

7. - We have found it helpful not to evaluate anyone's illness or recovery. *We recommend those struggling with the program to keep coming back to give our way of life a chance to work for them.*

8. - We use the "tools" of the program to recover - the 12 Steps, meetings and fellowship - Our Higher Power works through these avenues.

9. - Sponsorship aids us in our recovery. We can't recover alone - our sponsors can provide a better working understanding of the program.

10. - *Knowledge* about the inner workings of our OCD *does not* produce recovery. Our program doesn't address why we got our particular "brand" of OCD —it addresses how to recover from it.

11. - Our change in attitude results in our change in OCD. We need to be open to program suggestions so we can make the necessary changes in our lives for recovery.

12. - Working with newcomers is the backbone of our recovery. We stay well by spreading our recovery program

What is An OCA Meeting Like?

A healing occurs in our meetings which seems to defy explanation. If you are a member of another 12 Step program you are already familiar with "program" meetings. *The following are OCA's suggestions for a meeting:*

1. - Reading of the Preamble, To Those Of Us Who Are "New" to OCD, the 12 Steps of recovery, and Helpful Suggestions.

2. - An individual in recovery (suggested definition page 105) shares how it was before OCA and how he implements the OCA program for recovery. Often this person will read directly out of the OCA approved literature to reinforce his discussions.

   Other variations include step meetings (reading and discussion of one of the 12 Steps) or topic meetings such as resentment, control, perfectionism, willingness, Higher Power, etc.

3. - The meeting is then usually opened to those members who wish to share (participate). We have found it helpful when sharing to stick to the topic of discussion, but anything may be said by anyone (please respect our 12 Traditions). Crosstalk is discouraged - each member participates without group feedback. (If he chooses, the speaker may comment briefly after each member). We stick with the program's solution for us - we do not fuel our OCD with lengthy discussions of our symptoms.

4. - OCA has no dues or fees but we do have expenses. We pass the basket for those who wish to contribute.

5. - Close with the Serenity Prayer for those who wish to join.

The Twelve Traditions of Obsessive Compulsive Anonymous

1   Our common welfare should come first; personal recovery depends upon OCA unity.

2   For our group purpose there is but one ultimate authority — a loving God as He may express Himself in our group conscience. Our leaders are but trusted servants; they do not govern.

3   The only requirement for OCA membership is a desire to recover from Obsessive Compulsive Disorder.

4   Each group should be autonomous except in matters affecting other groups or OCA as a whole.

5   Each group has but one primary purpose — to carry its message to those who still suffer from Obsessive Compulsive Disorder.

6   An OCA group ought never endorse, finance, or lend the OCA name to any related facility or outside enterprise, lest problems of money, property and prestige divert us from our primary purpose.

7   Every OCA group ought to be fully self-supporting, declining outside contributions.

8   Obsessive Compulsive Anonymous should remain forever nonprofessional, but our service centers may employ special workers.

9   OCA, as such, ought never be organized; but we may create service boards or committees directly responsible to those they serve.

10   Obsessive Compulsive Anonymous has no opinion on outside issues; hence the OCA name ought never be drawn into public controversy.

11   Our public relations policy is based on attraction rather than promotion; we need always maintain personal anonymity at the level of press, radio, and films.

12   Anonymity is the spiritual foundation of all our traditions, ever reminding us to place principles before personalities.

The Twelve Traditions reprinted for adaptation with permission from Alcoholics Anonymous World Services, Inc.

The 12 Traditions of A.A.

1. Our common welfare should come first; personal recovery depends upon A.A. unity.

2. For our group purpose there is but one ultimate authority — a loving God as He may express Himself in our group conscience. Our leaders are but trusted servants — they do not govern.

3. The only requirement for A.A. membership is a desire to stop drinking.

4. Each group should be autonomous except in matters affecting other groups or A.A. as a whole.

5. Each group has but one primary purpose — to carry its message to the alcoholic who still suffers.

6. An A.A. group ought never endorse, finance or lend the A.A. name to any related facility or outside enterprise, lest problems of money, property and prestige divert us from our primary purpose.

7. Every A.A. group ought to be fully self-supporting, declining outside contributions.

8. Alcoholics Anonymous should remain forever non-professional, but our service centers may employ special workers.

9. A.A., as such, ought never be organized; but we may create service boards or committees directly responsible to those they serve.

10. Alcoholics Anonymous has no opinion on outside issues; hence the A.A. name ought never be drawn into public controversy.

11. Our public relations policy is based on attraction rather than promotion; we need always maintain personal anonymity at the level of press, radio, and films.

12. Anonymity is the spiritual foundation of all our traditions, ever reminding us to place principles before personalities.

The Twelve Traditions reprinted with permission of Alcoholics Anonymous World Services, Inc. The opinions expressed on this material are those of OCA only and not A.A.

How to Get in Touch with OCA

Our National Headquarters can currently be reached at (516) 741-4901 or write:

OCA
P.O. Box 215
New Hyde Park, NY 11040

Anyone who has OCD who wishes to start a meeting in their area is encouraged to do so. Remember OCA's message is the 12-Step program and how it can help us recover from OCD.

A meeting place is the first thing a meeting needs. Public meeting places such as houses of worship, libraries, schools, and hospitals usually have rooms for reduced fees.

Finding people to attend a meeting is the second concern. The following is a list of ways we have found each other:

1) Contact OCA. Let us know where your meeting is and the telephone number of the contact person for the meeting. OCA can then spread the word.

2) Contact the OC Foundation. Although not affiliated with us, we have a spirit of cooperation in helping those with OCD. The Foundation has a list of people who are looking for a fellowship like ours.

3) Local newspapers have sections where "community news" or "service groups" are mentioned free of charge.

4) Contact your local self-help clearinghouse — let them know your group exists.

5) Contact professionals in your area who have OCD clients.

6) Put flyers in post offices, libraries, or other meeting places.

7) Be patient. Most groups have found it takes many months to establish a core group.

Resources for OCD

1) **OC Foundation**
   P.O. Box 9573
   New Haven, CT 06535
   (203) 772-0565

2) **OCD Association of the National Capital Area**
   P.O. Box 11837
   Alexandria, VA 22312
   (703) 237-2407

3) **OCD Information Center**
   Department of Psychiatry
   University of Wisconsin/Center for Health Sciences
   600 Highland Ave.
   Madison, Wisconsin 53792
   (608) 263-6171

4) **National Institute of Mental Health**
   9000 Rockville Pike
   Bldg. 10 Rm. 3 D 41
   Bethesda, MD 20892
   (301) 496-3421

5) **COPE Publication (Literary Support Group)**
   P.O. Box 2361
   Ashland, Kentucky 41105